THE
ROAD TO THE HIKE
OF LAKE HAIYAHA

THE EXTRAORDINARY TALE FROM
AN ORDINARY GIRL

LAURIE TRAVIS

PAGE PUBLISHING, INC.
New York, NY

First originally published by Page Publishing, Inc. 2018

ISBN 978-1-64298-690-7 (Paperback)
ISBN 978-1-64298-692-1 (Digital)

Printed in the United States of America

This book is dedicated to all the ones I love—you know who you are and where you are—to family and friends that own a piece of my heart forever. Thank you for showing me the way, having faith in me, and making me believe again.

Magical moments lead to magical days that will lead to magical times. Belief is all you need.

Introduction

"I sometimes thought of you kids as being like a string of firecrackers. You were all strung together tightly. You were exactly alike, from the outside at least. You were all made the same. But you light those fireworks, and they all have different directions and reactions."

"Some are bright and beautiful, and at times you go 'Oohhhhh' and 'Aahhhhh.' And some of the fireworks are uncontrollable and dangerous instead. You'd scream 'Look out!' and end up in an emergency room when you light them. Of course, in every group of anything, there is the occasional dud. You light them and nothing. You don't get what you were expecting or even what you were hoping for on that firework. But that is also what makes you love those fireworks. You never know what you are going to get when you light them, but it's always worth the risk. There you go, Elle, there's your opening line."

This is what my Dad said to me when I told him at one of the many family occasions we got together that I wanted to write a book about our family. I told him that I thought we had some really good stories to tell about growing up in a big family that was very close and always active. So many stories about living in the Midwest in the '70s and '80s and beyond.

Just our family vacations as children would fill a whole chapter easy. Not to mention the holidays, all the summers on the farms, plus all our camping trips, family time, and the drama—oh the drama, good and bad—that always seemed to follow six children around. It would be a book that a lot of families would relate to and enjoy or at least find entertaining.

My Dad encouraged me to write that book and to gather stories from my brothers and sister, to do it while I still could because life can change in an instant. I put his quote on the backburner of my mind, remembering it and promising myself that I would write a book someday and use that line.

I just always felt like there was more to the story still. We had not reached our grand finale yet, something suitable to round out the book and end with. The story of our family will never really end; nobody's does. If it does, that is a real tragedy because all is lost then. So as long as the Garzo blood moves forward, our family story will continually be changing and building. The family tree will sprout new branches over time.

I had this conversation with my dad a good ten-plus years ago. There has been a lot to add to the story in that time. There is enough for several books because when life lessons come, they sometimes come in floods. I finally got the ending to my book that I had been waiting for. It happened. I told people about it. They were moved, touched, entertained, and it always ended with them telling me that I had to write a book about it, that it sounded like a movie-of-the-week story.

Then out of the blue, it hit me like a brick. There it was. My ending to my book. Why didn't I see that before? What was wrong with my thought process? Of course, this was the ending! It is an amazing tale that was given directly to me for a reason. I really feel it will not only entertain you, as any good story should, but will change your way of thinking, maybe even some of your beliefs.

It has some of those cliché, "If it did not happen to me, I would not have believed it" kind of moments. But I need you to believe it. I am not a writer per se, so forgive me in advance for all the grammar errors and the bad punctuation. I am a big fan of commas, I have come to learn, see what I mean?

I am a fifty-year-old woman who has been in retail management for twenty-five-plus years. I have not had an extraordinary life in any way, but a good life here—born and raised in Nebraska. I am the youngest of six children—four boys and two girls. We are very close not only in our hearts but in age, with only eight years (almost nine) between the oldest and I. My parents have been married for sixty years. I am as Midwest in values and as down to earth as you get.

This book is mostly about the last ten or so years. I will save my "growing up in my family" book for another time. I am an artist—I have been all my life—so I know when the creative juices are flowing, you have to go with it. I have to purge this story and share it with the world so I can move on, so I can grow and heal from this period in my life.

I will graze some of the stories of growing up to lay the foundation for the main event, but you will have to get the guts of those stories at a later date. I promise it will be worth the wait. I will also include some of my favorite *quotes* as well as some of my journal entries from this period of my life. I have been *journaling* for a large part of my life and believe in the release and peace it can help you to achieve. There is great power in words.

So here it is. I invite you to join me on this adventure. It will be a fun ride and, I recognize, at times a little hard to believe. You may have the opinion of many skeptics and think that I saw what I wanted to see or that some of these events are just a coincidence. But I *know* for a fact what I am asking you to believe is as real as this world gets.

Buckle in as we go on this trip together. There will be some good; there will be some bad. I hope you laugh and cry and take something with you that will help you in your own journey of life. Let's face it—life is really hard! We all have our coping mechanisms and do the best we can to get through and learn our life lessons. But it can really suck sometimes!

But above the pains of life, may you allow yourself some faith that, at the end of it all, there is good. At the end of it all, there is love. That is, in fact, the only thing we can take with us when we go. Love.

Chapter 1

The Bread

Our family is like branches on a tree. We grow in different directions, yet our roots remain the same.
— Unknown

When I was actually sitting down and starting to write a book, it was, to say the least, a little intimidating. Who am I to think I can write a book? Yes, I have journaled and written in the past, but a whole book? I found it less daunting to break it down by categories and subjects, to think of it as building a story. Creating a painting is like that; you learn to look at it in layers.

I read a lot, and one of my favorite authors is Stephen King. He has said a story should have a setup beginning, a meaty middle, and a big bang finish! It helped me to think of this project as a sandwich for some reason. (I know. Artists' eye roll, right?) So this first part is the bread, the bread or the base, if you will, just the basic parts that are holding the whole delicious story together, an official introduction to the Garaczkowski family.

That's my dad's name, of course, and so I will also be introducing you to the Koslers. My mom's side of the family and the side we spent the most time with. That is just usually how it is with married families, I have found.

Usually, one side takes priority for whatever reason over the other, either because of being geographically convenient or attitudes of families. There are lots of reason for this and many family dynamics that come into play. Both my mom and dad come from big families as well, so it only goes to reason that the larger the cast, the more drama in the play. Let's begin. Ladies first.

My mother, Madonna Matilda, is the oldest of seven children. She always had an exotic beauty with intense sable-brown eyes and dark-brown hair. I always thought she was the prettiest mom at the pool or in the room. She recently turned eighty years old and is still very active. She plays cards, goes to the casinos, travels, and helps in her church. She is very busy and has a full schedule. She comes from good genes and strong women. There is longevity there for sure. My great-grandma Matilda, whom my mom was named after, lived to be ninety-three. My grandma Loretta lived to be ninety-two and saw the year 2001! The changes she saw in her lifetime were mind-blowing. You recognized that when you spoke to her.

My mom was a kind, fun mom, and we had a loud and loving home. My mom worked in our elementary school as a building aid once I was old enough to start school. One of her jobs was to decorate the office and classrooms for the holidays. She decorated our home as well. We celebrated every holiday—I mean, *every* holiday. We had decorations for the big ones like everyone else, like Easter, Fourth of July, Thanksgiving. But we also celebrated Groundhog Day, Presidents' Day, you name it, even leap year!

I can still remember the April showers, umbrellas on the wall with raindrops coming down all over, and of course, the May flowers that came the next month. It was always fun with bright, festive decor all the time. It was the creative environment where we all got our imagination and artistic roots from. My mom ran a tight ship though; she had to with six kids. We were disciplined back then. We respected and healthily feared our parents. My mom could stop any of us in our tracks with just a look. We did not get away with anything, and the thought of entitlement was not even on our radar. They were different times indeed.

I watch those genealogy shows on TV and wish I had a whole network and team of researchers to help me with finding out my family history. Oh, the dirt we could find! But, alas, I do not. I have some information that different members of our family have discovered and put together though.

My mom recently put it all in one document and gave us all a copy. It was a good tool to use for this book and came at the exact time I needed it. Later at a family reunion, as I was almost done with the first run of this story, my cousin made a book with some more information in it too, not to mention some great pictures in her book. I am very lucky to have been blessed with such a close family. The precious memories we all received from those times are what made us who we are all today. The book was helpful and very timely. That is a common theme you will see in this story; the universe has a way of pushing things to you when you need them.

The Kosler family came over from Germany in 1860 when my great-great-great-grandfather Harm arrived. His wife died on the trip over, so he arrived with only his daughter, Anna, and son Hermann. He left to save Hermann from being drafted to the armies of the Prussian king. His other two sons, William and Henry, followed in 1864 at the ages of thirteen and ten. They lived on Harm's farm until 1874, when the boys moved to Iowa.

We have always been good people who work hard and value our family. The only semiscandalous thing I found was that our name was erroneously changed to Koesler from Kosler (no *E*) in 1880 when Harm passed away. The story goes that a neighbor in the cemetery had the same last name, so the engraver mistakenly spelled it Koesler. Harm's sons continued to use the name spelled Kosler though. How is that for German pride and gumptions? That explains a lot actually.

For the most part, until really my mother's generation, the family was of farmers and cattlemen in the Midwest. An impressive fact I read was that my great-grandfather William spent sixty-eight of his seventy-eight years on the same farm in Iowa. He was a very successful Hereford cattleman. There have been three Williams in our American family. My grandpa was William III. My own grandparents spent most of their lives on a farm as well until they retired and moved to town in Harlan, Iowa. We spent many days and nights on their farm, and I have some amazing memories of their hard work, good food, and clean country life. I miss them both very much.

On my grandmother's side, the Woerdeholf family was also from Germany. They can be traced back in Germany to the sixteenth century. They were farmers and appeared to have worked under the system where they paid tithes to a lord or nobleman. Conrad, my three-times great-grandfather, migrated to the United States in 1843, and they bought farmland and settled in Iowa. In 1870 Conrad died from pneumonia, leaving his wife, Margaret, to tend to the land with her sons.

My great-great-grandfather Aloysius (Louis) and his wife, Philomena, moved to Carroll County, Iowa, to start a farm of their own in 1873. Their son, my great-grandpa Louis, married Mary Resinge in 1911. They had four children, including my grandma Loretta, the oldest. At age forty-nine, Mary died of complications from gall bladder surgery, leaving my sixteen-year-old grandma to care for her younger siblings.

My grandma's strength was always obvious. I believe this is a lot of the reason why. She always gave us lots of hugs and love and was the best cooker of what is called comfort food ever. Her bread was amazing! My mother tried to recreate it once, using the same recipe, but it just was not the same. Grandma had that touch. My grandparents' farm was one of my favorite places to be when I was a child.

My father, Roy James, is the youngest of nine children. He has one sister and seven brothers. He is more of the light-haired, blue-eyed all-American type. I definitely got his eyes and looks. It is interesting that of us six kids, we kind of split the parents in the looks department. Some of us are dark featured, and some of us are light featured. All of us are beautiful though, if I do say so myself.

My dad was a handsome, tall young man when he entered the army. He had kind, gentle eyes and a sweet smile, especially considering how difficult his young years were. He lost his own father when he was just twenty years old, so he had to be the man of the house when he was quite young. The army was a good way for him to build a life for himself and my mom. When he got out, he started working in a pharmacy before working for the telephone company. He retired from the phone company after years of supervising. He took very good care of his family and always made life an adventure for us.

As far as a Dad goes, there are not enough words to say how lucky I am. He could not have been a better Dad to us if he had tried. I was always a Daddy's Girl and was fond of my dad's nickname for me: Elle, short for Elle-Belle. My dad had my heart from my first breath and will have it until my last breath. He is my main man; not even Santa Claus could compete. He worked hard and taught us to play hard too. He fished with us, did sports with us, took us every-where, and was the first one I would come to for advice. He's the smartest man I know and my hero.

My great-grandfather Stanislaus Garaczkowski came to America in 1855 from Poland. Stanley's father moved the family to Poland from Germany in the 1840s to escape the German draft, much like my mother's side of the family. When his father came in to Poland, he changed his name from Wagner to Garaczkowski. Of course, why wouldn't you, right? But then again, Garaczkowski was probably like Johnson in Poland. I actually really love the name and had great fun with it while growing up!

So on my father's side, I found again …not much scandal. In fact, I found some of the opposite. Stanley ended up in Lemont, Illinois, where they eventually helped found the Holy Family Church in 1897. Spiritual faith was a very important part of the family obvi-ously. One of my memories of my grandma Victoria was hearing her recite the rosary in Polish in the morning and nights. Like my mothers' ancestors, faith and family were important parts of my dad's heritage too.

My grandfather Joseph married my grandma Victoria in 1910. They lived with Joseph's family, and they helped work on their farm until they bought their own land in 1916. They were very good farm-ers and helped four of their own sons acquire and work profitable farms as well. They retired from farming in 1944, but my grandpa didn't retire from work. He worked as a painter up until he passed away in 1953 in his Armstrong home. I never got the chance to meet my grandpa Joe, and my dad did not get enough time with him. I feel devastated for my dad that he lost his father so young. I can't imagine how different I would be as a human being if I lost my dad at that age. Devastating.

Unfortunately, I do not have a lot of information about my grandma Victoria's side of the family. Maybe that is where all the scandal is hiding! They were Midwesterners and farmers as well though. As you can see now, I come from some really solid roots. This is basically the reason I am giving you the history of where my parents' lineages come from.

We did go see my grandma in Armstrong, Iowa, quite often. She always had chocolate chip cookies ready for us on the porch. She was an amazing cook and had the most sugary cereals for us. Franken Berry, Captain Crunch …she was the best! I remember she called my dad Jimmy, the only person I ever heard call him that. It was very sweet. My dad loved his mother very much. We all did. *Boz Padagosta Naz Dome*, Grandma!

Family Christmas picture, 1967, left to right, top row, Sandy, Scott and Steve. Bottom row, Laurie, Mom, Mark, Dad and Dan.

Now that you have met the lead players, my parents, the ones who started this branch of the family tree, I will introduce the rest of the family cast: my brothers and sister.

In order, we start with Steven James, the oldest son, the first-born, the child that had entire photo albums dedicated to him. He was a good-looking kid and was smart. He had the blond-haired, blue-eyed looks that got him opportunities. Steve had the gift of being smooth from a young age and has had a very blessed life. I am not saying that in any bad way; it is just the fact. We all have different paths. He married his college sweetheart and had a pretty daughter, Stephanie. He was divorced when Steph was a teen and was fortunate enough to find love again.

He is an executive in the construction business and has lived in some very different places in the United States, anywhere from Hawaii to Minnesota. He was always the kid any parent would be proud of. In fact, I don't really remember him getting into any trouble as a kid, teenager, or adult. Maybe he is just better at hiding it than we were. His new wife, Lyn, and he have a dog named Morgan, who has been the hit of the party whenever they bring her around. They have a very good life together and find adventures in their own travels.

Next came my sister, Sandra Kay, named after my dad's best friend, Kay, whom we visited in Colorado while growing up. Sandy is a dangerous beauty. She has my mother's exotic dark features and can flash her eyes in a way that will make a grown man nervous. She is very strong in her features and demands attention when she enters a room. She has always been thin and attractive, just like my mother. My sister married a mistake that luckily brought her an amazing and beautiful daughter, Angela Marie (named after yours truly).

My sister is also my friend. She is the keeper of my secrets. We shared a room when growing up and had so many conversations in the dark that nobody will ever know. We played ABCs when we couldn't sleep, a game only she and I know because we invented it. Her daughter was more like my little sister than my niece. The family calls us the "girls," which we love. Some of my most favorite lifetime memories are with my girls! Angie now has a precocious daughter of her own, my great-niece Aurora Kay. She is creative and funny and owns a large acreage in my heart. My sister has worked in service and retail most of her life. She keeps a clean, amazing home, and I look up to her and enjoy the time we spend together, like only sisters can. She is kind and caring and has a patience with people that I admire.

Now comes Scott Joseph. Here is what I know about him, a weird thing to say since he is my brother, but you'll see what I mean. He grew up with us and seemed like a normal part of our family and was fun to hang out with. We watched *Star Trek* together every Sunday night and had some good times. He joined the Army, and eventually he was discharged. It was of the nonhonorable type. He moved home and ended up dating a girl I went to school with, which is how they met (another common theme you will see). It was a very tumultuous relationship to say the least. He always stuck with her though, even over his own family sometimes.

When my grandpa William died in 1988, it was one of the last times I saw my brother. He didn't come to the funeral. At that point, he had already started to separate himself from the family. We, the kids, confronted him after the funeral. How could he do that to my mom and grandma? My brother Dan and I went over to his girlfriend's house and learned he had some demons he needed to work out. I will save for later the details of that story. I will just say that I only saw him a couple of times since then, and they have been confrontational and disturbing. There is much he has missed out on, both good and bad. He has done some unforgiveable things that my parents have forgiven him for but I have not. I don't have to. A parent's love is unconditional, not a sibling's love. I consider him the dud of the string.

Daniel Lee is the next of the boys. Dan is the brother who teases you just for walking in the room. If you tell him the sky is blue, he'll argue that it's periwinkle. Growing up, when we got in trouble, there was a good chance Dan was behind it. But that is what makes him so fun to be around. He is funny, loud, unpredictable, and he makes you uncomfortable. He is a party boy! He has dark hair and brown eyes. He is a handsome man with a big contagious smile. He is the combo of my parents in the looks department. He is most like my mom though, stubborn and strong-minded.

He is always 110 percent into whatever his most recent thrill is; whether it be bodybuilding, biking, skiing, Dan was all in. He started to date one of my best friends while I was still in high school. (See? Here we go again.) They ended up moving out to Denver together after graduation. They eventually broke up and have separate lives, but they remain friends to this day.

He is one of the most creative, talented artists I know. He has been a professional custom framer for over half of his life. He currently does the framing for an artist in Colorado on her original work for her galleries. Dan has had his difficult times in life like everyone else. But my brother has been blessed with some good luck and must have a herd of angels watching over him because he always manages to land on his feet.

I have always spent a lot of time in Colorado, and it has a very special place in my heart. I spent a lot of time with my brother those first ten or so years he moved out there. I have really funny memories of our times together. We did some crazy things and one-of-a-kind adventures. We laughed until we cried and talked around the campfires when we camped. He always made it memorable. I am sure you can guess which firecracker he is, right? (Sound of ambulance sirens.)

The last boy and closest to my age is Mark William. Named after William III—my grandpa, of course. Mark has my father's blue eyes and light hair. His eyes are very kind and inviting and make him quite beautiful. He was always long legged and tall with a barrel chest. He has deep-set dimples that never went away. He would be mad at you and cussing you out, but his dimples would be so adorable you could not take it too seriously. All of my friends thought he was hot!

Growing up, Mark always tried to include me. I was always the annoying little sister following her brothers around, trying to play with them. But Mark would play with me when he could. When we were both in high school together, he would have to drop me off or give me a ride home before I got my own driver's license and car. It was during one of those pickups that my friend Rachel and Mark first saw each other. Well, if you have been paying attention to the story, you'd know what happened next. What can I say? My friends were all very cute! Mark and Rachel ended up marrying. I was in the wedding, and I wore the prettiest red dress I have ever worn. Unfortunately, their marriage ended as well. It was a double bummer for me because not only was I sad for my brother and wanted to support him but I lost a friend too.

Mark never really found true love again. He was with a woman for a short time. She had a baby girl, and he was blessed with a daughter, Brittany. He had a brief relationship with Brittany's mother, who had another son from another man. My brother was such a stand up; he's the do-the-right-thing kind of guy that he ended up adopting the other child, his son, Brandon. His relationship with their mother ended, but he continued to support the kids. That is the kind of man Mark is. Brittany has also made him a grandpa two times with her two adorable sons, Bentley and Lincoln.

Mark has spent most of his life working as a printing press operator. When I think of my brother, I think of nature. When I think of nature, I think of my brother. I have never known anyone who was so in tune with nature and wildlife. His personality is kind, quiet, and respectful, but you don't want to make him angry; that's for sure. There is not a better man than my brother Mark, except for my dad.

This brings us to the youngest of the children—me! Laurie Marie. I was what you would call a "happy accident." But my sister would call it the best day of her life! Can you imagine being the only girl with four brothers? I have always been creative, and learning comes easily to me. I consider myself witty and fun to be around. I have green-blue eyes and blond hair. I definitely take after my father.

I passed on two art scholarships out of high school because I just didn't want to go to school anymore. My parents let me make that decision and live with it too. I went to college a few years after high school, though, when I could afford to pay for it. I was working in a very popular Mexican restaurant and making good money. I was still with my high school boyfriend, Eric. We ended up moving in together and were together for twelve years before getting married. It was a destination wedding in Jamaica, and quite frankly, that was the only way to get us to get married. We were content just being together. But sometimes people shouldn't get married. We were separated within a year and divorced within three.

I was one of the lucky ones who found love again though. I married my second husband, Greg, over ten years ago in the Colorado Mountains. We eloped and surprised everyone. It was beautiful in the Rockies as always, and that December, they had received many feet of snowfall leading up to our trip. Our cathedral was under two enormous pines and surrounded with snow and nature. It was a gorgeous, sunny mountain day and perfect. We have a good life together and are great friends as well.

I have been in retail management for over twenty-five years and like the work. I still have friends from high school that I cherish; it's so good to get together with them. Every once in a while, you should have people around you that knew you when you were young, knew you when you were a teenager doing dumb teenager things. They know the truest you that there is, our immature selves, the version of us that feels things like we will never feel again, sees things like we will never see them again, has the courage and invulnerable attitude of an adolescent who thinks they will live forever, and are still experiencing life lessons for the first time, having high moments and low moments like we never will again in our lives, when our walls have not been fully built yet. Sometimes I miss that *me*.

I can't mention our lives and characters without talking about pets. They were always an important part of our lives. We had too many to even list. We had a pet cemetery in the garden that was full of hamsters, gerbils, guinea pigs, fish, pigeons, and rabbits among others.

The first dog I remember was Whimpy, who got his name from the first night we brought him home and the action that followed. Can you blame him? He was missing his mommy? He was a little tan short-haired mixed breed with a curly tail, like a pig, which was fitting since he was a little on the full side. He got a lot of table scraps from the kids. We had Whimpy a long time, and he was my very first introduction to losing a "family" member. Yes, we had lost many little pets but not a dog; he was one of us. He camped with us, played in the yard with us, went fishing with us. He was a part of the family and a playmate of mine. His death helped prepare me for my grandma Victoria's death the next year. I still remember my dad sitting on the front porch with me, explaining how when we lose the ones we love, we will see them again so we never really lose them and that we will love each other after death too. It comforted me at a time I was devastated about my grandma's death. Thank you, Whimpy, for that life lesson; it eased my grief a little.

Our next dog was Smokey, who was a dachshund-terrier blend, a very cute, strong, fun dog. We took long walks together when I was a teen. He knew some of my secrets and was a good listener. It was hard to lose him; he was a good friend. When my brother Scott graduated, one of his friends gave him a puppy. We named it Keggar, and it, of course, became my parents' dog. He was a beautiful midsize black-and-tan dog who was not the brightest animal I have known but was a good boy. Keggar was the dog who retired with my dad. My father retired several years before my mother, so Keggar was his buddy every day. They were good pals. He moved with them and lived on the lake when they both retired, and he spent his final years with my dad and mom there in paradise.

After Keggar died, my parents could not bear to have another dog. My dad said it was too hard on his heart. He had always told me that a dog was a cruel joke on us from God. Because we would never experience such unconditional, real love that was guaranteed to leave you. We would always outlive our dogs, he said (maybe not always).

Just a couple more pet highlights in the family. I always wanted a horse more than anything in the world. Every birthday and Christmas, my parents would ask me what I wanted, and the whole family would say with me, "A horse." And then they would say, "Now what do you want that we could actually give you?" So no, I never got my horse. But my parents always gave me a horse something, like a horse stuffed animal, horse statue, horse color book, etc. even as a young adult. I still love horses and their strength and beauty.

We did have a bullfrog named Jeremiah (sing the song now if you remember it); someone put an M-80 into him while we were in Seattle for the Fourth of July. He was all over the inside of his box. Poor guy and gross! We had a white rabbit named Angel. She lived in a hutch in the backyard, and it was always a treat when my brothers said I could feed her. My brother Steve raised pigeons in the garage, and I think he still has not forgiven me for the time I got mad at him and broke some of the eggs. What can I say? I knew it would get him where it hurts. That is what little bratty sisters are for, right?

I had many hamsters, but the one I loved the most was Tony. He was my favorite! I had been told I could not play with him as a form of punishment once, so I snuck him into the bathroom to play. Well, my mom knocked on the door, and I panicked and put Tony under the sink. After my mom left the bathroom, I looked under the sink, and Tony had crawled between the floorboard and sink pipe down below. I could not reach him! I had to confess to my parents what I did.

They sent me to bed, and I cried myself to sleep because surely Tony was gone forever. I woke up in the morning to the squeak of Tony's exercise wheel going around and around. Tony was saved! My dad had worked all night to get that little pet out. He had to saw the floorboard so it opened up more and he could reach down and get him. All I knew was, my dad was a hero! I did not care how he did it, but he saved my hamster! In our house, pets were family, and we loved them as such. All of them. I am so grateful that we were raised this way. It has brought so much into our lives and has given us an appreciation for all the animals on this planet. As adults, we all have pets as parts of our families, and we always will, until our hearts cannot bear it anymore too, I guess.

Chapter 2
The Spread

Mom told me to go outside and play when I was little. Thanks, Mom.

— Anonymous

Now that you have tasted the bread of the sandwich, let's get to the spread, the part that gives it adhesive, making it so you can put on the rest of the ingredients without the risk of them falling off. That way, it is not just boring, dry bread. Have you ever tried to make a dry sandwich? All the meat and cheese moves around so when you take a bite, it slides right off. You need something to hold it all together. The spread. Now I prefer using butter, but feel free to make your sandwich that is being built in your reading mind with whatever spread you prefer.

I am kind of a plain Jane girl when it comes to food. As little kids, we would go to McDonald's or Burger King through the drive-thru as a special treat. This was before the days that we could "have it our way" or before "special orders don't upset us." So we would have to pull over to the side and wait for my *plain* cheeseburger. It drove my brother's crazy, but that is the way I like my cheeseburger! The fact that it drove them crazy was just a bonus! So here is the spread. This will help hold the rest of the story all in place. Here are some highlights of growing up with this bunch of knuckleheads before I get to the meat of the story.

We were living in Westgate, a suburb of Omaha, Nebraska, when I was born. I only lived there until I was three years old, so I don't have a lot of memories of it. It was a cute little house with a white picket fence. The backyard had a fish pond, sand box, and swing set with red-and-white striped poles. It was a child's dream play area.

One very vivid memory I will always have is while we were still living in Westgate, a tornado hit the Omaha area. I remember being out on somebody's shoulders—my uncle Bob's, I always thought—and being able to see the tornado. It was a classic V-shaped twister, and the impression it made on me was very strong. Obviously, I can still remember it so clearly even after almost fifty years.

My parents built a new house in the Millard area in 1968. In fact, that tornado I remember so vividly actually put the construction of our new home back due to the damage it caused. Luckily, we were not in it yet. Or who knows what the outcome would have been? Timing is everything. Millard is another suburb of Omaha. My parents always liked to live on the edge of town and let the city come to them. We built a house on a circle, close to our junior high and elementary schools, and that was also very close to my dad's work. It was a bigger home and a great neighborhood. In fact, I live in Millard again. I bought a house there a few years back.

There were four other families living on the circle with us, and everyone got along very well. The Rosenblooms and Edgarts are my parents' lifelong friends. They still keep in contact. We all had kids about the same age and played together constantly. The youngest Rosenbloom boy, Mike, was my very best friend and only a year younger than me. We grew up together and were inseparable. There was a pool down the street that we could walk to, and our elementary school was also within walking distance. It was an amazing place and environment for me to be in during those very formable years of three to twelve. Not to mention it was also the '70s, so those were rapidly changing years in the world and pop culture too.

Those were simple and fun times, a childhood everyone would be blessed to have. We played kick the can and hide-and-go-seek. We had a vacant lot next door that we played kick soccer and baseball in. There was tree climbing done and four square to be played. We had a basketball hoop in the driveway; most everyone did. We walked everywhere! To school, to the pool, to a friend's house. My best friend Mike would knock on the front door and ask if I could come out and play. He usually interrupted our dinner. And yes, we had dinner together every night.

The boys all shared a room until we finished our basement. Can you imagine four boys in bunk beds and the fighting that came? My sister and I had always shared a room and did until she moved out. We did not always get along, but it was nothing like the crashes that came out of the boys' room. Eventually, we finished the basement, and the two oldest boys moved down there.

It was also the perfect set-up for tornado watching. We could be in the driveway, and if we saw a tornado coming, we could run in the garage that led right into the basement. Living in Nebraska all my life and that extremely vivid memory of the tornado I saw when I was very little have desensitized me. I grew up thinking that unless you see a twister coming down your street, you are safe. This is not true, as I found out later in my life. I was awoken in the middle of the night with a sound that sounded like a jet plane coming down on us. I now have a respect for tornados that I did not have before, but that's another story.

We spent the weekends as children, camping and fishing together, as a family. I remember when I was a little girl I was some-times upset that I could not go to a friend's house for sleepovers. I always had to spend the weekends with my family in nature. What a pain! I was getting dragged to different lakes and fishing spots or another campsite in a different state. I am so grateful for that now. I did not know it at the time, but that was building my lifelong rela-tionship with nature.

Our family used nature and being in it as a way to relax, as a way to bond together and with the elements. As a young adult, my solo trips to the mountains were what helped develop who I was and who I want to be. I was taught to pause and appreciate all that Mother

Nature has to offer. I did not learn that from watching TV or playing video games. I learned it from being loaded into our wood-paneled station wagon with the camper being pulled behind it and going on a weekend adventure or a week-long road trip to somewhere we have never been before. We had our favorites, of course, too. Minnesota, South Dakota, and Colorado were regulars for us. The free time my parents gave up taking our little troop on camping and fishing trips is so appreciated by us all.

I have a million stories about growing up during these times: our first microwave, mine and Mike's matching purple bikes, hooking Aunt Bev's nose while fishing, my brothers' stitches, my other brothers' stitches, I could go on and on. See why I said I have several books to write still? One story that is mandatory to tell you now, though, is the glasses story.

On one of our trips up to Canada, my sister lost her glasses, and they were new glasses, of course. So here is what happened. We were cruising down the road, and my sister was hanging her head out the window, catching some wind, when …*whoop!* Off go the glasses! The look on her face when she pulled her head back in was one of pure shock and fear. That was it. Her time was up! She lost her new glasses. Here we were on our way out of the country, and Sandy could not see a thing. She was too terrified to say anything. Here we are, cruising down the highway and getting farther and farther away from her glasses, and she still is not saying a word. Pure terror had paralyzed her.

So now us siblings started teasing and saying, "Mom!" And she says "What?" And we say, "Oh, nothing." And we'd start laughing just to freak Sandy out. See what my poor parents were up against? Finally, my dad, sensing that something was up, demanded to know why we were laughing. That was it. Having no choice, Sandy fessed up that she had put her head out the window and lost her glasses.

The breaks screeched, and the wagon pulled over.

"Where?" Dad asked.

"I don't know. Back there," she answered. The station wagon was turned around, and the search began.

"Do you remember any signs or anything you saw before they came off?"

Of course, not. She was free in the wind, feeling the breeze on her face. That always seems to be the times I feel most nervous— when everything is awesome! Brace yourself. Here comes life!

It was a slow crawl back on to the highway as we retraced our steps. A little cussing, a little praying, and some hiding, just to stay out of the sight of the fury. Well, I told you that I had the best dad in the world, so are you at all surprised that, yes, my dad found those glasses!

He spotted them, pulled over, and picked them up. He was always my hero, and now I fully understood why. There was nothing my dad could not do. After inspection, we also realized that the glasses were fine. Not a scratch! A vacation miracle! The trip was saved! Dad tucked his Superhero cape back under his shirt and got the station wagon and his little army back on the road!

A year to remember was 1975.

One reason is, it was the year that one of my all-time favorite movies was made. *Jaws* changed my life forever! I saw it at a friend's birthday sleepover party. We all had to get permission to go from our parents. There were a couple girls who did not get to go. My parents let me go, and I thank them very much! I am crazy about scary movies, and this was the mother of them all.

It made me scared to swim in lakes, rivers, even at a hotel swimming pool in Oregon that summer. We were on our way to Seattle, and I swear I saw a dark shadow in the deep end! Of course, I was swimming alone. Don't judge. It was the '70s, and I was an excellent swimmer. Frightened, I hightailed it back to the hotel room. My parents questioned why I was back so soon, and I told them the water was cold. I could not tell them it was because of the great white shark! I would never be allowed to go to another scary movie.

That was also a memorable year because of the January 10th Blizzard of '75 too.

The forecasters got it wrong. No such thing as Doppler radar yet, kids. They had predicted four inches of snow, and we got over fourteen. School was not called off; everyone had gone to work. It was a mess! I remember Dad got stranded at work, and Mom was stuck with us all alone. Six against one—not good odds. She kept us entertained though. We made homemade ice cream! We just opened the front door, scooped some snow out of the wall of snow that had drifted in front of our door, and we were ready! It was fun and delicious!

My dad eventually walked home. There was no getting around by car, not for a few days. The unexpected storm had caused over ten thousand cars to be abandoned on the streets. We went outside to play the next day, and that was one of the only times in my life I had been really scared of snow. I was little, and there was a lot of snow! I got stuck a couple of times. The storm killed fifty-eight people, fourteen of which were in Nebraska.

That was also the year of the May 6th Tornado of '75.

Seriously, can you imagine? Two once-in-a-century storms in the same year, only four months apart!

The tornado started forming above our house. The sky was a bizarre green-grey color that everyone in the Midwest knows as the tornadic activity color. We were, of course, standing in the driveway, watching the sky, playing basketball as the sirens were going off. But then we noticed a slight rotation in the clouds that made us run to the safety of the basement.

Our house was not harmed in any way. We were lucky. An F4 tornado ripped through the city, killing three people. At times, it was over a mile wide and skipped and bounced around, leaving a trail of debris. The next day, we all piled into our station wagon to go viewing. Only this time it was not to go see Christmas lights; it was to see the destruction of a once-in-a-lifetime (fingers crossed) tornado. There is something so bizarre to see one house completely leveled and the house next door barely missing a roof shingle. You may think that we were out seeing the misery of other people and being lookie-loos, and we were to a point. But we were also being taught to respect Mother Nature because she ultimately will get the last word and has unlimited power.

The year 1975 was also the year that my oldest brother graduated from high school and moved out to start college. That was the start of the birds starting to leave the nest, and as a little girl, it felt strange to have a family member not in the house anymore. It's not like I was particularly close to Steve. I thought his friends were cute, but I was going to miss having him in the house. Everyone carries an energy with them, and now we had one less energy in the house. I think I started to realize that year that as time marches on, things in life will always change. I am sure it was eye-opening and bittersweet to my parents too. They were nothing but supportive, but I am sure some tears were shed as well.

We spent a lot of time growing up with my mother's side of the family. They were mostly farmers in Iowa and lived close to one another. With the exception of two of my mom's brothers, they were all in the same area. My grandparents also lived there too, and they were only an hour away. We spent holidays there, reunions, and birthdays. Or we just went to visit on the weekend. I had twenty-six cousins growing up, and we were all about the same ages, so I always had country cousins to play with. I was especially close to my cousins Karen and Cheryl. We were all only years apart and had great fun together.

We lost Karen to cancer when she turned forty. It was heartbreaking. But her funeral was amazing and huge! There was standing room only. As I sat there with the family, I thought about our times together as young girls, and I cried. I cried because I was so very proud of the woman she became. Look at all the people she had touched! It was amazing!

As we stood outside the church, my cousin Denise and I laughed together. She said, "Don't expect this kind of turnout at my funeral." And I agreed. "Yeah, don't worry about where you are going to park or sit at mine. I will be lucky to fill a section, much less a church." We cried and hugged and looked in the sky and told Karen how impressed and lucky to be her cousins we were.

Grandpa William and Grandma Loretta
at Christmas, Harlan, Iowa.

The holidays with my mother's side were always a blast! We all filled my grandparents' house and went down to the basement to open presents. It was a madhouse, loud, unorganized, and so much fun! We did holidays traditions you only hear about in songs. We went caroling around the small town, and people gave us hot cocoa and cookies for our songs. I admit, I was sometimes asked to not sing.

Let me tell you something about myself: I *love* to sing. But I have no voice. I have always been told that. As a young kid, I would be running around the house, singing, and my mom would say, "Laurie, Laurie …please go outside and sing."

But in a cruel twist of the universe, I have automatic recall of songs I hear. I can sing along with the lyrics after only hearing it once or twice. So unfair! Plus, I *love* Christmas songs! Year around!

Another holiday tradition I can say I did was a one-horse open-sleigh ride! It was snowing and there were Christmas lights; it was magical! These memories are the reason that even now, I really love the Christmas season. And I work in retail, so I don't really get a Christmas break. But I still believe in Santa Claus (wink) and Christmas snow.

Another memory growing up with my mother's side was the summers we spent at the farms. My parents have been married for sixty years, and that's not luck—that's work. With six children, one thing they knew was that eventually we would all go away and they would be alone again. So they worked on their love; they nurtured it.

One way they did that was for two weeks every summer, they would run away from home! They would go off on their own vacation and leave us with our grandparents and aunts and uncles. We would bounce from farm to farm and wear out our welcome then move on to the next.

As we got older, they would divide us up. Pretty sure that was my aunts' and uncles' idea. We were a lot to handle. This was when our grandparents were still on their farm too. I loved our summers on the farms! As far as I know, our parents did not check up on us very often. They did their thing, and we did ours. We were naughty, so I am sure they got the phone calls about what we had done now. Good thing for them that was before the cell phone era.

Mark, Laurie and Dan playing in a pile of
corn on the farm, Harlan, Iowa.

We wouldn't do anything too bad. Let the cows out in to the yard. Maybe jump in the corn silos, and tease the pigs. Fall out of a tree. I do remember a couple little fires in the barns, but nothing major. We really had the best of both worlds—city life and farm life. Each farm was different. One uncle raised sheep and bred St. Bernards, so there were always puppies and lambs to play with. Another had pigs, another cows or corn. And you want to talk about dark? Try being outside in the middle of Iowa with no lights on except the yard light. You could see so many stars you had to look for the black in the sky.

Another advantage of being on the farm—and I am talking about both my mom's and my dad's side of the family—was the food, obviously fresh, fresh, fresh. We had homes we were on that were dairy farms, so we had fresh milk. Fresh eggs, fresh vegetables, fresh meat—they were all just outside our door. Plus, the baked foods.

As I said, my grandma Kosler made bread like nobody else. I could sit down with butter and eat a whole loaf. My aunt Dolly on my dad's side made the most amazing cinnamon-and-orange rolls! Little flakes of orange zest and homemade icing, holy moly! They were so great, and she always made them when we visited. When I graduated from high school, she made a batch and shipped it to me as part of my gift. Most delicious and thoughtful! My grandma Garaczkowski made the most delicious cookies, chocolate chip, and there were fresh batches every time we came. She had really good breakfast too. Her eggs were delicious, and she always got brown eggs. For some reason, that made it yummier for me.

We spent plenty of time with my dad's side on their farms too. My favorite was my uncle Dave and aunt Dolly's farm not only for the cinnamon rolls in the morning but because they had a pony! My cousin Bruce was always charged with taking me on rides through the apple orchard when we visited. He confessed at my parents' fif- tieth wedding anniversary party that he was always told by my uncle Dave that he had to stay on the farm when we visited so he could take me on my ride. He said he always fought it and resented the fact that he couldn't go hang with friends. But when I was on the back of the pony and he was walking with me and he saw the look on my face, it was always fine. He enjoyed it in fact.

The biggest spider I have ever seen in my life was on this farm too. I had gone down to the barn to do a chore (yes, we were free labor on all these farms too), and there on the wall was a barn spider at least a foot long! In my little imagination, it was three feet long, of course, if not bigger. I ran back to the house and my cousin Tommy went back down with me. But it was gone. I have had a major, almost unrealistic fear of spiders since that day no matter what the size.

At my uncle Walt and aunt Katherine's, I remember all the fireflies in the summer! Just hundreds of them lighting up the night! It was not hard to collect them in a jar to make your own flashlight. I also remember the adults playing cards and yelling. It was a fun and teasing yelling but seemed so out of place in such a quiet environment as the farm.

Being at my grandma Garaczkowski's during the holiday was always special. We always celebrated our own family Christmas on Christmas Eve in Omaha. We were told that Santa made a special trip to us so we could open our presents early. That way we could drive to my grandma Victoria's for Christmas Day. Grandma didn't do a lot of decorations for the holidays, but I do remember my favorite. She had a little two-foot ceramic Christmas tree that she had in her window. It blinked and glowed, and I remember falling asleep in front of it every year. Some years there would be Christmas snow falling too. Those are heartwarming memories.

My grandma always had parakeets. They were blue or yellow, and she could take them out. Of course, the one time I tried to do that, it flew away and up to the ceiling. I got in trouble for that one. Grandma was talking polish. She was so mad; that was never good. She taught us one Polish phrase: "God bless our home." She had a framed picture of it that was hanging in the dining room, and it was a part of our prayer every meal. I still remember it to this day, and my mom made a cross-stitch of the phrase for all of us to hang in our own homes.

The kids at Grandma Victorias, left to right, Sandy, Dan, Laurie, Grandma Victoria, Mark, Scott and Steve, in Armstrong, Iowa.

The relationship my dad had with his mom was very special to see. All his brothers also had a very close relationship with her. Those boys really loved and took good care of their mother. My uncle Fat (yes, that's what we called him and he was okay with it) was a life-long bachelor living in the same area as grandma and checked on her often. He took her to church on Christmas Eve and Easter. Going to church in Armstrong was so spiritual. It was a small town with a small church and big church bells. When church was starting, you could hear it for miles. Christmas Mass was especially beautiful. It was the same church my own parents were married in.

My uncle Fat was a sweet, formidable man whom everyone adored. We spent time with his other two brothers, Walter and David, and their families too. They all lived in the same area as my grandmother. My dad also had a close relationship with his much-farther-away brothers. We went to Seattle to see Uncle Pete and then to Rome, New York, to see Uncle Paul. They were twins, and when they were younger, the brothers would call them Pete and Repeat. I think that is hilarious! We also went on a road trip to Arkansas to visit Uncle Clarence. My dad's only sister, "Sis" (Clara), was in West Virginia.

They all also came to visit us in Omaha a couple of times. The family bonds were very strong on both sides of the family, and there was always a lot of love. I felt secure in that thought as I grew up. Children need to have that to feel safe, and I know that I am fortunate to have those feelings as a base for my growth. It set me up for those inevitable changes in life.

When I was thirteen years old, I had the rug of my life pulled out from under me!

The first *major* event in my life that I remember physically and mentally changing me happened. We were moving! We were building a new home in what was now West Omaha, and I would start a new school—a junior high school to be specific—the start of the "big leagues," the final trot toward graduation.

All my friends that I had gone to elementary school with for the last seven years (including kindergarten) would be going to a different school than me. I would be starting my teenage junior high school life not knowing one single person! No friends who knew me, grew up with me, spent summers with me, made me who I was at that point in my life. All gone! I was devastated!

The summer before seventh grade was the hardest in my life. But it was also the start of some of the best times in my life.

I was all alone for the first time ever. I always had a neighbor or friend I could go hang out with. That was gone now. But my parents threw us a bone, so to speak. They put in a backyard in-ground pool. The pool would not only make me less miserable, which it did. But it would help me to make new friends, which it did. Let's face it, it was an amazing party house!

I also had a bigger, better bedroom and nice new bathroom that we all did not share. After only a couple of years, my brother Scott went into the service, so even my brothers had their own rooms for the first time! It was a good move. But it was a traumatic move. My grades really failed that first year, and I went into a funk for sure. Nothing my parents could not help me out of though. Plus, of course, I was an adolescent; that was not helping anything.

I made some neighborhood friends that summer. That was a good way to start the school year; at least not every face was new. They were not what I would call good friends though, those I met in eighth grade.

I met some in seventh, but our little "gang" did not really come together until the next year. We were best friends all through high school, and I have some of my best life memories with these girls! We had so much fun, got into some trouble, had lots of tears of laughter and pain, experimented together, shared secrets and love! Through the magic of Facebook, we all still keep in touch and get together when we can. I am still very close to a few and have enjoyed our adult relationships very much.

As you can guess by now, because of the frequency of my brothers dating and even marrying my friends, I was a pretty girl growing up and had cute friends. Birds of a feather, I guess. I was, as I later found out at a high school reunion, one of the hot, untouchable girls. We were the cool girls! Who knew? I always thought we were popular, but untouchable? Do you ever think that if you were aware of your power while a teenager, how dangerous you could be? I was so insecure about my looks, always covering up my 36-28-36 body with sweatshirts, flannels, baggy Levi's. Just imagine the damage I could have done if I had the self-confidence and self-awareness that I had in, oh, let's say my thirties.

The dynamics of my family completely changed as I grew older and started to hang out with my brothers and sister in a different way. I was more of a peer than a little sister for the first time. Their friends actually wanted me around when they came over. I had some big crushes on some of my brothers' friends, but we never acted on it. Some kissy, feely stuff, but nothing beyond that. I was a teenager after all.

But we all got closer and closer as we aged. We would go to concerts together, party together, even go on sibling vacations. We spent time camping and going on road trips. My bond with my two brothers Dan and Mark became very strong in high school and beyond. We were the last three at home and had a lot in common. My bond with my sister was always, and always will be, the closest, but our history is totally different.

When Dan and my friend Ann moved out to Denver, I spent a lot of time going to see him. Not only was I going to see my brother, but my friends would go with me too so they could see Ann. Could you blame me though? Colorado has always been my most favorite place on the planet, and now I had a free place to stay there. It was only an eight-hour drive and worth every minute. I was dating my high school boyfriend (and first husband) Eric, and he would go as well sometimes. He and I would go out there by ourselves too. We all got along very well and made great memories. This was back in the more carefree days—before mortgages, car payments, and a fifty-hour work week.

As I said, Colorado has always been a special place to me. I spent a lot of time there with my entire family, with a friend, with my brothers, and on the most important trips of my life, by myself. It was the home I had come back to even before going there for the very first time.

During my thirties, I went to Rocky Mountain National Park outside of Estes Park many times by myself. These are my most precious trips, and I always came back with a better understanding of myself. The first time I played with the notion of going out there by myself, my parents, especially my dad, were against it. They were concerned for my safety. I was too, of course, but I felt it in my soul that it was something I absolutely had to do. I had to test myself and my bravery.

That first time, I actually called my parents from Estes Park and told them that I had gone. I know I was in my thirties, but are you ever too old to be worried about by your parents or worry about what they thought of you and what you're doing? I assured them I would be safe. I told them my plans day by day, called someone every night, and would leave a note in my room as to which trail or area of the park I would be in for the day. I had my pepper spray for bears. I knew mountain lion safety. I was a mountain girl after all!

These solo trips to the mountains were the instrument to my discovering who I was as a human being. It helped me become friends with myself. If you have never had private time with yourself, quiet time with your feelings, and inner voices as your only company, I recommend you do. You do not have to do anything drastic and as dramatic as me. Not everyone should go to the mountains all alone.

You can just go for a long walk, spend the entire day by yourself, no distractions. It really helps you clear your mind of all the outside noises and problems and puts you back in tune with yourself and the rhythms of life. I call it scrubbing my soul. Nature, as I said before, was the way I released stress and appreciated life. It helped me relax and enjoy all that the planet earth has to offer. I have been taught this from a very early age, and I am eternally grateful for that.

I love going to the mountains alone because it is *my* trip. I can pick whatever trail I want and go at my pace. I can take as long as I want by a stream and just be quiet. I can spend hours drawing or painting on the side of a mountain lake. I have had adventures and seen views that only I understand. I have had encounters with wildlife that would never happen if I was with somebody else.

I have also had beautiful, aawww-inspiring moments, like leaning on my car while twenty feet away a group of deer crossed the road. It was spring, so there was young deer with their own road-crossing styles, anywhere from running out of control across the road to nonchalantly taking their time across. It was a beautiful moment that made me laugh and cry at its innocence and purity. On these trips, I feel very in touch with nature and all it has to offer.

Once I was sitting by a stream, a babbling brook, for a good hour, just enjoying the sun and mountain air, when all of a sudden, a huge bull elk came crashing through the brush right on the other side. He didn't know I was there because I was being so quiet.

(Actually, that is a big no-no when in the mountains alone by the way; always make noise). Well, he gets a drink, looks up right into my eye, and at this point, we are about five feet away from each other with only a narrow stream between us. We were so close I could see my reflection in his big black eyes. He does not feel fear, and oddly, neither did I. He moves along at a slow pace, never really paying any more attention to me. I sat there, watching him move along, and I cried. That is why I go to the mountains by myself—for those moments that will propel me from dark life moments when we are tested, to inspiring life moments that are wonderful.

In one of those trips, I had climbed down to an area in what they call Rock Cut and sat on some massive boulders. I was out of view of everyone there. I had the mountains to myself! It is a tundra area and above the tree line. The views of the fourteen-thousand-foot mountains are breathtaking! There is a particular range you can see there that is beyond majestic. You can almost see how those magnificent mountains were formed and the hugeness of their existence. You feel immensely small in their presence.

There is an amazing alpine lake you can see from there that I call Laurie Lake. I know its actual name, but I will always refer to it as Laurie Lake. My entire family calls it that now. I have been admiring this lake from the very first time I visited the park in my teens. There is something magical about it. On this particular day, I made a decisive, serious decision. I wanted my ashes spread right there when I died. Not at the lake, although that would be amazing yet nearly impossible, but right near where I was, in its shadow and view. In that moment, I thought that I would finally be home.

When I got back to Omaha from that trip, I told my parents about that decision. I was only in my thirties, but they took it seriously. My parents made notes about where and assured me it would happen if the time came. I even wrote it down and put it in my lockbox so my final request would be carried out. Our next family vacation out there, I showed them where it was.

I had been to Estes Park with my brothers several times and had even stood with them right at Rock Cut Point. They knew exactly where I wanted to be spread. This was not the first time my brother Mark and I had this conversation. It was just the first time it felt so official when I told my parents.

When I was still in high school, I went to Rocky Mountain National Park with Mark, Rachel, and Eric for a camping trip. We spent one of the days, as we usually did, driving to the top of the mountains to the visitor center. We stopped frequently and took in the awesome views behind every bend of the road.

Hiking off the road, we could and were really enjoying the mountains. When we got to Rock Cut, my brother Mark had said, "There's Laurie Lake." I told him someday I would get to that lake. Maybe only my ashes would be spread there, but I would get there eventually! This was when I was just a young woman, so it was an almost flippant remark that I later decided was very serious.

My brother had taken it seriously already though. He thought it was a great idea! What better way for us to still be in harmony with nature, with the mountains that we loved. He had said that if I promised to spread his ashes in the park, he would spread mine.

I giggled and said, "Okay, but where do you want yours? Good luck getting to the lake too by the way."

We laughed about it, and he said he would tell me where he wanted his ashes when we got there and he saw it. I said that was fine, but he knew where mine were supposed to go.

We didn't say anything else after that promise and conversation. He never told me where to spread his. I never asked how he was going to spread mine. We were young and having a great time in the mountains and living life! But we had the unspoken bond and promise that we had each other's back.

Life is long, and there was still time to hash out details. But I had his, and he had mine. I knew he would never fail me, and I would never let him down. Even if I was an old woman whom someone had to drive out to the park and help because I was not capable of doing it alone. That is what you do for family. That is what you do for the people you love.

The next big dynamic change was when both of my parents finally retired and they moved. They had always said they would retire on a lake in Minnesota and my dad would drive a black truck and have a boat again. And they did it! Big time!

They built their dream lake house in 1990 on Lake Latoka in Alexandria, Minnesota. The most gorgeous A-frame house with all glass windows in the back, facing the lake. The sunsets from their deck were some of the most amazingly beautiful sunsets I have ever seen in my life. And they just repeated their splendor night after night.

The view of Lake Latoka from the deck of my
parents' house, in Alexandria, Minnesota.

It had a loft where us girls would stay when we visited. Of course, they had lots of company who stayed there, but we always thought of it as ours. We had a paddleboat, two docks, a swing loveseat, a fire pit, and a fast fishing boat! My dad bought himself a big black Dodge

Ram truck as promised. We fished; went swimming, intertubing, and skiing; drove the boat around the chains of lakes; and sat in the sun, soaking up the rays. We loved our lake and every moment we got to spend there. They were living the life they had always wanted, and we had the ultimate vacation spot complete with home cooking!

The years my parents lived on the lake were some of the best of my family's history. We had so much fun going to see them every time. We missed them dearly and looked forward to each time we got to be close to them again, but we were proud that they were living the life they had always planned for. We even had Christmas there for the first few years. It was so beautiful, and we were always guaranteed a White Christmas! We would sled and ice fish, have hot cocoa; it was very scenic and traditional. My brother Mark got stuck up there because of a blizzard one year he stayed later than us. Then my parents decided to be snow birds and come to Omaha for the holidays and down to Arkansas until March. The winters in Minnesota are as rough as they are gorgeous.

When I first realized they would be seven hours away, I was so scared. They were my safety net. My rocks and constant support that I always knew I had. They would still be all of that, but I couldn't just stop by to see them or have dinner or just go over for a hug and talk because life was kicking my ass. A visit with them always made things better. How would I cope now? I coped by growing up even more. I coped by cherishing every moment with them that I could. It is a strange thing. I was born and raised in Nebraska, but when I went to the lake, I always thought of it as "going home."

Because it's not just a cliché—home *is* where the heart is. My hearts lived on a lake in Minnesota now.

When we went to the lake, it was a major stress reliever. I could feel the stress melt off me with every mile north. We had our routine, starting super early to get there for lunch. We stopped in Sioux City or Sioux Falls for breakfast at a drive-thru. When we got to the lake, after hugs and kisses and hellos, we would go down to the lake, say hello to the water, and go back to the house for lunch.

After lunch, it was boat time! Us girls would take it alone, and we would also cruise around with the parents too. Dad always had the boat gassed up and ready to go. We would spend most of our day on the lake then go in for a family dinner. I was the driver of the boat when we fished because I didn't have the patience to fish. I was always asking Dad if it was time to find a new spot. Should I move the boat to the other side of the lake? Should we go to another lake? I had no patience, as you can tell. Do not really have it now either.

Since the mosquitos ruled the dark in northern Minnesota, nights were for dominos, cards, and board games inside. There was always a lot of laughter and singing and teasing and love. We played hard on the lake and then rested up. We slept like a rock and ate like crazy. Homemade cookies and cinnamon rolls were a must at every trip. We always grilled hot dogs and s'mores over the fire pit. It was the best that life had to offer. We were so fortunate and spoiled to have this time with the people we loved in one of the most beautiful places.

I made some very big decisions at Lake Latoka. I had many talks with my dad on the dock and got sound advice and frank talk from both my parents. When I watched the sun glitter off the blue of the lake and listened to the waves lap on the shore, it eased my mind.

It made things clearer and hard decisions obvious. It was always so hard to leave when it came time to do so. It was hard to let go of my parents, and I cried every time. Yes, I would miss my lake, but it was also obvious as we drove away that I was leaving my heart there too. I missed my parents being so accessible. I missed the affection and human touch. It was always good to talk to them on the phone, but nothing is like a hand hold or hug.

When my parents decided to move back, I was torn. Obviously, I was thrilled to have my parents back in Omaha, but what would I do now that I couldn't go to my lake? It was the place I needed to de-stress and feel like I was on vacation and recharge my batteries. I would not be able to just run down to the dock, jump in the boat, and take off. I wouldn't have the relaxation of lying on the boat and feeling the waves rock it back and forth as the loons cried their haunting cry. When I jumped into the lake and swam, the water was always cool and refreshing. Sitting on the swing as the waves broke on the shore, I saw amazing sunsets. I would miss sitting on the swing watching the sunset each night.

I was grateful that I had the time up there that I had, but it was not enough. The love for lake life was formed in us at a very early age, and we lived it for real for all those years. What now?

I still remember vividly that last morning at the lake. I remember standing on the dock with my sister, niece, and Dad and we were just hugging one another and crying, just staring at the water and loons floating on the top. I was bawling my eyes out. None of us wanted to leave. It was the last time us girls would be on that dock at our lake.

We got jars from Mom and took some of the sand, rocks, shells, and lake water with us. Walking away from that body of water still hurts my heart now to think about. It had become such an important part of my life and who I was that it literally pained me to face the reality that it was not our lake anymore.

It was a long drive back to Omaha, and there was not an hour that went by that the whole car was not crying again. It would hit us like a train again and again. We were not going back there ever again. We would all have it together and stop the tears. Then someone would bring up another memory, and there it went. We would start to bawl. We were grieving for the lake and for that part of our lives being over. It was the saddest drive of my life.

My own selfishness aside, the timing of my parents' return to Omaha was a blessing.

Living on a lake is a whole lot of work, and my parents had had enough. Although they loved it very much, it was hard on them to maintain everything necessary to have a boat, docks, and large home that had many visitors year around. My parents were always gracious hosts, and many of my aunts and uncles as well as some of my cousins would visit often along with my parents' friends too. They had a calendar with everyone's visit logged in; at times, it looked like a bed-and-breakfast schedule.

It was hardly an easy retirement, but it was an amazing life. The timing was perfect because just two years after their return, my dad had heart bypass surgery. It was very scary, and we were all so thankful that they were here, in Omaha, where we could be with him instead of five hundred miles away.

Before my dad's health issues and directly after they moved back to Omaha, we took our final family vacation together. My parents bought a caravan, and they took Sandy, my niece Angie, Mark, and me to Denver, where we picked up my brother Dan and went to Estes Park. We stayed in a lovely house in Castle Mountain Lodge with a small cottage separate for the boys. It was a good time and a mountain adventure. We saw a black bear in the resort one evening and had lots of hiking and exploring area just outside our door. We drove through the mountains, saw Laurie Lake (of course) and all the stunning scenery the mountains have to offer. I will be honest; there were some fights too, but that is what family does.

One of the days, us kids decided to take a long hike. So we all drove up to Bear Lake and hit a trailhead. The plan was, my parents would walk around the more hiker-friendly Bear Lake trail and we would head in to the mountains and hike up to a Glacier Lake. We picked Lake Haiyaha trail, which we called lake Haiyayayaya … hahaha (laughter, which was required every time). It was a two-and-a-half-mile hike and would take us a good four to five hours.

The hike to Lake Haiyaha on our family vacation.
Left to Right, Mark, Laurie, Angie, and Sandy.
Rocky Mountain National Park, Colorado

We all grabbed our backpacks, butt bags, trail food, and walking sticks, and off we go. I have been on many trails in these mountains, but it was the first time I had done this one. It did not disappoint—breathtaking views in every direction and clearing. Wildlife was present in the form of Elk, deer, marmots, and many birds and critters. It was a perfect mountain day with that unreal blue sky that makes you feel closer to the clouds. It was a challenging hike and good for beginners at the same time.

We had a great time and created some amazing memories together. On this trail, the first lake you come to is Nymph Lake. It is full of lily pads and flowers and just gorgeous. It looks and feels like something out of a fairy tale. There is this huge piece of tree that has fallen over and dried out and makes a great photographic opportunity. You can stand in front of the dried-up roots at the base of the fallen tree, and they are a good fifteen feet wide and spread out very aesthetically to the eye.

We wanted to have a picture of us there. I happened to notice this very beautiful man, and I decided to go ask and see if he would take a photo for us. He was blonde haired and blue eyed and Swiss looking. As I asked him, he had a European accent and was even better looking up close. We flirted, and we stared at each other even as we walked away. It is obvious to see the smile on my face in the picture that we were smitten with each other at first sight. Even though I would likely never see him again, I fell for him.

My brothers, of course, teased me the entire trip. They called this mystery man Sven—Sven from Sweden. They would say things like "We just saw Sven at the grocery store" and "Wait, is that Sven over there? Oh no, that's not him" or "Laurie, I think Sven is at the door or on the phone." They teased me endlessly. I secretly hoped that we would run into Sven in some restaurant or store. But we were meant to not see each other again. That young man added to our trip and made it even more memorable and fun. He was completely oblivious to his contribution to our family vacation that year, nor was he even aware of how he impacted our lives even after that vacation and years later. The memories of that hike are still very strong.

It was one of my favorite days in one of my favorite places with some of my most favorite people.

That was our last family vacation together, and I am grateful that it was somewhere that I still frequent to this day. There are so many great memories everywhere I look. It is a special place and therefore worthy of our final chapter in family vacations. It was the place where I got married years later. It is a place where some amazingly powerful things have happened. It is a place that has the touch of beauty that comes from Mother Nature only. It is a place where you can ground yourself spiritually and energize yourself mentally. The Rocky Mountains of Colorado have a tie with me and my family that at this time is now unbreakable.

The last family vacation in the Colorado Rockies. Left to right, Dad, Sandy, Mark, Mom, Dan, Laurie and Angie.

In the year 2004, my parents celebrated their fiftieth wedding anniversary. We had a huge party! It is a proud occasion and one that most people never get the chance to celebrate. So we had to do it good! We decided the kids would plan it all. All my parents had to do was just show up. What that translated to was, my sister, Sandy, and I planning a party.

It was actually very fun. We went all out and were very creative with our party ideas. Feel free to steal any of these ideas for your own party. We duplicated their original wedding cake and then had a sheet cake with their original wedding picture scanned on top. We decorated to match the original colors of blue and yellow right down to the basket to put cards in. We sent out a request with the invitation to "Send your favorite memory of our parents to us" so we could put them all together in a decorated chest box for them. We had some great responses, and many people put them in the greeting cards as well, so they were an extra special surprise for my parents.

We had disposable cameras on all the tables so we could get the moments captured. We had Siamese fighting fish (betas) in bowls on the tables as a treat for our guests to take home if they wanted and to make it a different kind of centerpiece. There were balloons, confetti, and a trio of memory boards with pictures from the different eras of love. Everyone crowded around these. Us children all got up to say something and honor them. We had a limousine pick them up, take them to church for mass, and then take them to the party—then, of course, back home after the party. We spoiled them, and they deserved it!

Sounds so glamorous and wonderful, doesn't it? Well, it was. And it was a great party, one that everyone talked about for years and my parents' friends brought up in envy. We made our parents so proud of their children and how thoughtful we were. But here are some hilarious side notes to the party.

We had a family "meeting" with us kids the night before at my sister's to go over things. At least that was *my* agenda; everyone else was already in party mode. I wanted everyone to talk about their speeches or what they were going to say. I had mine all written down and rehearsed, and my sister had a poem that she wrote and was ready. My brothers Steve and Dan were going to wing it. Well, you can imagine how that made me feel …anxious. And Mark didn't want to say anything at all.

I kept trying to get everyone to focus so we could go over things, but nobody was listening. They were all laughing and having a good time. I was the little sister again and being ignored right before the big show! I was a nervous wreck! We had the helium balloons filled and ready to take to the hall in the morning when we decorated. They were at my sister's, and somehow when someone opened the door, most of them floated away. Nobody has confessed to that even to this day.

Even with the missing balloons, the place looked great. As the party started, though, something terrible began to happen. My cousin came up to me and said that the fish at her table had gone belly up. On no! Not the party atmosphere we were going for. I discreetly removed and flushed the fish. As I walked around to check on the others, I found other fish struggling. Throughout the party, I went around and collected dead fish and gave them a toilet burial. That was not in the plan!

We did end up with enough fish for all of us who wanted one afterwards though. I got one, and my niece, my sister and brother, my parents, and a couple of cousins all took one home. I have to admit; most of the fish didn't last very long. But my fish, Bubble Boy, ended up living for almost seven years! He was a good fish. We were living on an eight-acre pond at the time, so he was buried in that water and was spared the flush. RIP Bubble Boy!

When my sister and I went to develop the film of the cameras on the tables, we were disappointed. We got a few good pictures for my parents to have, but the majority of the pictures were of butts, the floor, close-ups of noses, feet, butts again. We forgot to factor in the kids at the party and what would happen if they got the cameras. We should have put an adult at each table in charge of the camera. Ooops!

Those little mishaps aside, it was an amazing party! The speeches all went well. There was laughter and tears, and my parents felt very loved that day. That was exactly the party we wanted.

The book we made for Mom and Dads' 60th Wedding Anniversary. The cover photo is their original wedding portrait.

My parents also made it to their sixtieth wedding anniversary! This is a huge accomplishment and one they are very proud of. We all are! We did not have the huge party this time around. Do you know how hard it is to find decorations for a sixtieth wedding anniversary? Very difficult, which speaks to its rarity. We had a lovely dinner, and everyone was able to make it. The whole family was together again for this very special occasion. It was a nice dinner with diamond-and-doves confetti, balloons, and pictures.

We went back to my parents and surprised them with some gifts. All of us kids had written down our sixty most favorite memories of growing up in our family. We all wrote down fifteen each. We were surprised at how many were duplicated and of the memories we had forgotten about but still meant a lot to another sibling. My sister and I then put them all together with pictures and created, with the help of our sister-in-law, a book. They were so touched, and they loved it! They actually ended up getting a copy for each of us the following Christmas so we could all have the book.

I wrote to the Vatican, and the pope sent an amazing ornate and beautiful letter congratulating them on their diamond anniversary. We got it beautifully framed for them as well. My dad especially was overwhelmed with this gift. The idea that the pope had given them his blessing and love was too much. We also had a letter from President Obama and his family congratulating them as well. It was a picture of the whole first family on official White House paper. Although Obama may not have been a favorite president of my parents—come on, it's still the president! You don't get a letter from him and the White House every day now, do you?

It was a really moving night and one I will never forget.

There was love, and that is all we ever need.

Chapter 3

The Meat

You never know how strong you can be until you have to be strong.

— *Bob Marley*

All right, now you have the bread and spread for your sandwich. Let's get to the meat of the matter or, if you are vegetarian, the *plant* of the matter. This is the part that will get in your gut and give you the energy and understanding you need to move on to the tastier stuff. Let's face it; the meat, although delicious, is the heart of the sandwich. It is where we get the protein and calories needed to survive.

It is also the fuel for our system. It creates those big poops that clean out the system. (Sorry, Mom, I said *poop* in my book.) Just like life, these "cleansings" sometimes hurt, sometimes take too long, and sometimes comes out of nowhere. That is just like our life experiences; they come when you need them. You don't plan them; they appear when you least expect them.

So let's get to the substance, the juicy part. Take a big bite of this and try to swallow it down. The tale turns now to a real-life middle.

This is by far the most difficult chapter for me to write not only because I am still a little fuzzy on all the details (I am sure a psychiatrist would say I am "blocking" these memories) but because they tear at my heart. My mom had actually kept a journal of the following events, but it was unfortunately lost. We are going on memory as far as dates and timing in some cases, but the actual events all happened.

April 6, Good Friday, 2007, was one of the worst Fridays of my life. there was nothing "good" about it, in my opinion.

But let me go back a few months first. On Father's Day in 2006, we were all at my parents' house for a celebration, grill out. We had a good time with lots of laughter and fun as usual. We sat down to dinner and began to eat our cheeseburgers and fixings. My brother Mark started to get the hiccups. They were so bad he had to excuse himself and walk away until they stopped and he could continue to eat. He told us it had happened a few times before but was not sure what it was.

Fast forward to Thanksgiving. We sat down to give thanks and eat the traditional bird, and Mark's hiccups started again. This time it was longer until he had them under control and could eat. We saw it again at Christmas too. He confessed that they had been coming almost every time he ate now.

We insisted he go get them checked out. His body was trying to tell him something. He said he would, but let's face it—he is a man, so he put it off. (Sorry guys, the truth hurts). It really was not until we all got together for my Mom's and my birthday celebration in March (our birthdays are two days apart) that we all got on him about getting it checked out. After that, my mom bugged him until he made an appointment with his doctor.

At the end of March, he had an endoscopy done to look down his throat to see what the cause was. They found tumors on his esophagus and removed them for biopsy. He was supposed to call for the results a couple days after that.

We all kept on him to call for his results as soon as they told him the date to call. He would tell us he left them a message and that they left him a message but they just had not talked yet. You can imagine how crazy this was making all of us! We were anxious and worried. As they say, the waiting is the hardest part.

On that Good Friday, both my sister and I happened to be off work, and Mark still had not received any information about his procedure results. So we decided to go over to his house, and we were not leaving until he had talked to the doctor. We had decided we did not want him to be alone when he talked to them either. Maybe this was why he was not calling too; we were all scared for him, so of course, he was frightened as well.

We drove over to his house and asked him if he had tried to call again. He said he had not but did not make a move to do so. My brother is a proud man, and he will do things on his terms, I have found. After hanging out and playing with his new puppy, Alpine, for a while, he got up and made the phone call.

He got through on the phone. He talked to his doctor. He got the results. He hung up the phone after making another appointment and came and sat on the couch with us. He sat there for a second, digesting what he had just been told. Then he told his two sisters.

He had esophagus cancer.

The room spun, and I left my body a little. I think they call it shock. But in front of him, I was strong. Both my sister and I were there for him. I was so grateful that we were. If he had to get the news alone, it would have devastated us. Everything happens for a reason; of this, I am sure.

We held hands. We hugged. We supported and encouraged. We cried a little when he did, but we were his rocks. We told him he could beat it, that he was super strong, and that he should not freak out until he met with his doctor and got his plan of attack! I think at that point my sister and I were freaking out enough for all of us—on the inside, of course.

After a while, we left. He had some phone calls to make, and the kids would be home soon. He would have to tell them and told us he would do it alone. We told him that as soon as we left, he had to call our parents and tell them. He said he would. We hugged hard said "I love you" many times, and then we got in my car to leave.

I barely got down the street after waving goodbye to Mark and Alpine who were standing on the front porch before I lost it! It was a meltdown! I found the strength to hold it together in front of Mark, but that strength was gone now. I was so amazingly scared and hurt and shocked by the news that all I could do was cry. How could this be happening?

Both my sister and I were overwhelmed by the idea of the fight he had before him. I would do anything to not have him go through this!

We called our brother Dan in Denver and told him the news. Dan is very emotional like his sisters, and we wanted him to have time to get his brain wrapped around it before talking to Mark. He was destroyed by the news. This was his closest brother, whom he shared a bedroom with for most of his childhood. He was understandably distressed and felt very alone out there in the Rockies. I felt terrible that we could not hug him and comfort him the way we could one another.

When we returned to my sister's place, we called our parents.

"Has Mark called you yet?" And they said no.

We told them to call him right away. We did not tell them anything; that was his job to do. They called him right away and got the news. I am sure they went through their own version of hell like we all did that first day. I can't imagine what it is like to hear that your son has to fight for his life.

Cancer had taken my grandpa, and now my mom had to watch it try to take her son. We hate cancer! My parents then called my brother Steve, who was living in Hawaii at the time, and let him know too. I had to tell my husband and friends and coworkers. Those were some of the hardest conversations to have. He was not alone; we were all in this fight. Now it was our new reality. Our world had changed.

That was my worst Good Friday, followed by my worst Easter.

I had always liked Easter; it's the beginning of spring! There's candy! There's family! There's flowers! When we were little, we would get new Easter outfits! It had some really lovely memories attached to it.

All gone.

Easter began to be and still is one of the hardest holidays for me to get through. The one following my brothers' diagnosis is still fresh in my mind. We tried hard to ignore the elephant in the room, but when we sat down for Easter ham, it was impossible.

There they were.

Those hiccups.

As we sat down and ate, Mark began to hiccup. It had happened to us many times before, but now we knew exactly what those nasty little hiccups meant. It was heartbreaking to us all. I still remember sitting at the table with Mark's daughter Brittany chewing through her tears. Mark was trying to eat, and she was quiet and eating and chewing her food with tears streaming down her face.

The day continued, and we all took turns crying—most of it out of Mark's presence or awareness. We all by instinct knew we had to be strong for him. But we could lean on one another and share those raw emotions together. We had to if we were going to get through this.

Mark met with his doctor, and he had a very aggressive plan of attack! Mark was a healthy, strong, strapping man of forty-five with lots of life ahead of him. That was all of our opinions. They would start with very high chemo and radiation treatment rounds. It would begin with six weeks of strong chemotherapy three times a week. He would also have two rounds of radiation at the beginning and end. My mother was the ultimate support and often drove him to his treatments and back home. Even when he was being stubborn and decided he didn't need anyone's help, my mother was there.

> *Call Mark about his test results, I need to make sure he knows he is not alone and pick up a card to send him, it's so hard. But how the hell do you think he feels, give me strength for him.*

These were very intense and painful times for my brother. I saw my brother struggle to get through the changes in his body and through the treatment, and I knew there was nothing any of us could do to help. This was Mark's fight. I would give anything to do it for him, but that was not an option. The treatment was killing a part of my brother very slowly. It is true that the treatment has to almost kill you in the process of killing the cancer.

He lost weight. He was sick to his stomach very often and was weak. As many of you know, it is one of the hardest things to do—watching someone you love in pain and fighting for their lives and you are helpless. There were times when I would go over and he would be on the bathroom floor, unable to get up. I helped him up, tried to make him comfortable, tried to get food in him, loved and supported him. Then I'd walk out the door and cry my eyes out.

I cried for him and for myself because being strong when I felt like crying, yelling, throwing something, and screaming how unfair it was, was my only option, the only way to help. But it sure felt good when I was alone and having a heated conversation with God and myself and the meaning of it all. It was a lot like grieving and had its different stages of coping.

But we continued to be strong for him. What choice did we have?

I went on major defense mode. Nobody was going to hurt my brother. I would make sure of it. I was there for him with everything he would need. The claws were out, and I was going to protect him from anything I could.

I bought everyone in the family Livestrong bracelets to wear to show solidarity in our family support for Mark. I mailed them to my out-of-town family members in Denver and Hawaii. The idea was that when we all wore them and when we looked at them, we knew we were all in this together. None of us were alone. We all wore them.

Now I am not saying there was not some cracks in the family because of this prognosis. There were. I can't imagine a family out there that has gone through this and not been affected and changed in some degree. Everyone reacts differently to this kind of devastating, life-changing news. I have learned that. But in my anger with this disease and the cards my beloved brother was dealt, I needed someone to be mad at.

So I found one.

Now I am going to tell you about "the letter" (cue dramatic music, doohn, doohn, daaa). After Mark found out his fate and began to start his fight, it took my brother Steve, in Hawaii, almost two weeks to call him.

In my eyes, this was unacceptable!

I have since learned that it may have taken Steve some time to live with this notion and how to deal with it. My brother Steve is an executive in his company and has always been the "boss." He is a problem solver and authority figure. This was not a problem he could solve. It was messy and uncomfortable and very emotional to talk about. He needed time for all that. I understand that now.

Now.

At the time, I was furious! I was livid with him and thought he was letting Mark down. "He didn't give a crap!" That was just what Mark had said to me one day, and that got me crazy!

I decided to tell my brother exactly what I thought about the way he was treating Mark. Finally …my target!

I knew he would never sit through a phone conversation with me yelling at him and having a heated discussion. My brother Steve did not like confrontation. Most everyone else in the family were very good at it, but not Steve. In his position at work, he rarely had people disagree with him and was probably never told he was doing anything wrong, he was good at everything he did.

I decided I would be the one to check him. I did not work for him. He was my brother, and I could say whatever I wanted to him.

I wrote a letter, telling him that I felt that he had no clue what was going on, that he was protected by the "big blue body of water called the Pacific Ocean" and did not have to see the things I saw when I went to visit Mark. He did not have to do the things we were doing for him, so the least he could do was pick up the damn phone and call him more often so Mark would know he cared!

There was a tone to it, and I was telling him exactly what I felt he needed to hear. Wrong or right, I was venting as well. Like I said, I was mad and finally had a chance to unleash.

Now I read this letter to everyone in my family. They all agreed with what I said. They would not admit it maybe, but they did. Even my dad had said I should send it. "He needs to hear those things" was what he had said.

So I sent it.

It started a mini battle. I do not regret it, but it caused some rift in the family for a short time. I am sure my brother ripped up the letter. He told my parents he was pissed about it.

But you know what? He changed a little. He called my brother more often. He even came to Omaha and spent the day with him. When he traveled, he tried to get a layover in Omaha so he could see Mark.

My brother Steve is a very good man, and I know now that it was just a very difficult situation for him to deal with. I am glad it all turned out for the best, and in some ass-backward way, the letter actually brought us all together. After a little while, of course. It takes time to heal every wound.

My brother Mark had some amazing support through his cancer treatment.

My parents were there for everything, and I mean *everything*. My sister and I went to see him every chance possible and took him to a meal once a week. I sent him cards every week or so, just for support.

Did you know that Hallmark has a whole section of cancer cards? From the diagnosis to the treatment to remission. I would go and pick out these cards, just crying my eyes out.

I got a lot of looks from people around me, wondering if I was okay. Was I? I do not think I was. I was fighting cancer right next to my brother in any way I could.

I would put little daily inspiration cards in there for him too. Positive thoughts! My sister called him a lot. She always had good advice and kind words for him—the big sister! My husband and I spent a lot of time over there, "playing with the puppy" and visiting.

Mark and Alpine in Council Bluffs, Iowa.

It was a special blessing that he got his puppy at roughly the same time he was diagnosed. Alpine is a Bernese mountain dog and a big boy. He gave Mark both mental and physical support. He is a good hugger and a strong dog to lean on when you need it. Plus, he always has a big goofy smile for you, and it is contagious.

My brother Dan called and checked in on him all the time. My brother Mark would say "There's Dan calling again" and roll his eyes, but he would smile the smile of love. He knew Dan cared about him and was thinking about him all the time. He felt that love even five hundred miles away!

My brother had good friends to help him through too. His friend Tony was a lifelong friend and was very close to our entire family. He had a very difficult time with the process at first, and it was very hard for him to see Mark in his condition. He called quite often, but as my brother got sicker and weaker, he had a hard time when he visited.

I did not fault him for that; it was a really scary thing to see.

My brother also had a close friend, Joe, who was a huge help to him. He would go over almost every day and check on him and get him what he needed. He lived closest to Mark, and we were all very happy to know he was just down the block. Mark lived across the river in Iowa, while we were all in Omaha except for Joe.

Both Tony and Joe would take my brother out when he was up for it too. They would go mushroom hunting, boating or to the lake. They did as much as they could to make sure Mark was still "living," that, yes, he was in a battle but that he was not going to sit and be sad about it. He would continue to do the things he enjoyed with the people he loved.

Mark had both of his children still living with him during this time too. They were teens and unfortunately had to grow up way too fast because of this terrible disease. They were there for their dad the best way they knew how and could. They both love their dad very much and tried to be as strong and supportive as they could.

But let's face it; they were teens whose dad was very sick. That is a lot to ask them to understand and accept. Life as a teenager is hard enough: trying to figure out who you are, what you want to be, who your friends are, not to mention the hormones. Dear God, the hormones! There were times that they really could not deal with it. I understand that.

It sometimes made me mad, protection mode and all, but I do understand it. There were times I left and wondered how I just got through that visit because it was so difficult. So I do get it.

He had a supportive team of nurses and doctors as well. They would make the best out of all the different, surely humiliating and humbling moments. They made him laugh and feel like they had his back, that this was their fight too! All that positive energy helped him in so many ways.

My brother's faith had his back too. He went back to church during this time. He would go every Sunday he felt strong enough. Remember, we were raised Catholic, and we all had a strong root in our faith. We all have our own personal relationship with God. My brother was taught to lean on his faith in hard times, to give thanks to it in good times. It was time to lean.

After the chemo and radiation treatments were over, he had a new scan. There was significant shrinkage of the tumors on the stomach and esophagus. But not enough. They would have to do surgery—and a nasty surgery indeed. The gist of it was, they would remove most of the esophagus and the part of the stomach where the tumor still remained. And then they would pull the flexible top of the stomach up and attach it to the remainder of the esophagus. That's the short story of it at least.

They waited a few weeks to let him gain some strength back, and then they scheduled the surgery. In July, he had surgery to remove the cancer tumors still in his body. It was a difficult surgery, and Mark was weak, but he made it through. He fought on!

Now came a new battle though—the battle of food. He was not going to be eating anything through his mouth for a time, so he had a feeding tube and bag attached directly into his stomach. He would have to get his nutrients through a tube for a few weeks until eating would work again. It was a process that he learned to do at home and went smoothly enough, but he was still losing weight. He would level off sometimes but never really gain any. That was always the one question he would not want to be asked but the one we all wanted to ask. "How much do you weigh?"

Eventually, he made it through this stage as well and began to eat orally again. His eating was going to have to change though. He had what they called a "slow stomach" now, and eating too fast or too much would make him sick and cause pain in his belly.

Now you need to understand, I come from a family of fast eaters. We had six kids and only so much food. You did not get seconds until all your food was gone. Sometimes there was not enough food for everyone to get seconds; thus, the fast eating skills were learned.

Mark also could not drink milk anymore. He could have other dairy, like cheese. But milk in any form—soy, lactose free, Ensure—those all caused him pain. Now I also come from a family of milk drinkers too. While we were growing up, my mom would cut our gallons of milk with water so it was half and half because we went through so much milk. This would be devastating to me! I live for a glass of chocolate milk! But Mark just made the changes he needed to make and learned how to live with his new body. He was alive! That was what mattered!

It was 2008, and my brother Mark was cancer free!

Growing up, Mark had always had different nicknames from his friends. Garzo was a name the whole family had, but they called him Shark because of his billiard abilities. They called him Frog or Toad because of his long legs and Wolf because …well, just because.

Lone Wolf was what he always called himself.

He especially embraced this nickname and persona during his cancer treatment. It was his and his alone to do. As much as we all loved him and wanted to help, he knew it was all in his power. On some of the long talks he had with my sister, she told me that she had written poems for Mark and had often read them to him. He had been inspired to write a poem himself, and she shared it with me. It is heartbreakingly beautiful.

Lone Wolf

Mark W. Garaczkowski

The air was cold, and the moon was shin-
ing bright,
The mist was falling, in the silent night.
Moving through the trees, not making a
sound,
Always aware of what is all around,
You can see the pain, running through his
eyes,
He has no pack, to recognize his cries,
Hunting alone, just to survive,
Killing what he can, to keep himself alive,
Forever free, forever he will roam,
Lone Wolf will always be alone.

The Lone Wolf beat cancer!

I could not have been happier or prouder of my brother. He showed strength I am not sure I could have found in myself. He was my hero as well as my big brother!

To celebrate this moment in his life, he got a tattoo, a permanent reminder of his win. It was a ferocious-looking, growling, snarling wolf, just like the cancer that just got its ass kicked by Mark. But it was also strong and beautiful, just like my brother. He wore it with pride and honor.

For the next two years, he got a scan every six months. All clean and cancer free. Then for the next three years, he was supposed to get a yearly scan. The five-year date is when most doctors will tell you is the point that you can say it is over. If it has not come back by then, it likely will not. So we held our breaths and prayed every time that scan would come up, and we were always blessed with clean results!

That brings us to summer 2011. He has been cancer free (since we counted the surgery as his cancer-free moment) for four years now. Mark had a scan, only two left until his final five-year-out-of-the-woods scan.

His stomach and esophagus looked good.

What they found was a cancerous tumor on his right lung.

Another punch in the stomach for us all. Just when we were feeling confident and almost safe, that nasty disease shows its ugly face again!

We were all devastated! How could this be. He had beat it! It took parts of him already, literally, and it had taken from all of us. He had played fair, followed the rules, and won!

How could this son of a bitch be back? He would start a new battle in the war for his life! I was crushed and heartbroken for him. New cancer. New doctor's appointment. New plan of attack to beat it!

Now this time around, Mark was not the strong young man he was the first time. He had gone from 175 pounds to 135, on a good day. He was over six feet tall, so he looked very thin in this new body.

He would be unable to do radiation because he had already had as much as they could give him his first round. He would need to do chemo again for three weeks, two times a week. Then they would have to strengthen him up and perform surgery to remove the part of the lung with the cancer.

The hopes were that the treatment would shrink the cancer again this time. We all wondered how this would be possible in his current condition. We all had hope but fear. Mark did not.

He had beat it before. Why not again?

He was pissed, and using that anger to fight was a great thing to see. He should be pissed! It was unfair, and he was not going to take it! He knew the routine; the fear of the unknown was not there this time. He knew how to beat it, and he would do it!

Again, I was blown away by his strength. Who was this man? My brother was sweet and kind and helpful to anyone who needed it. I would joke that Mark is the only person I know who back in the day would actually not hang up on the telemarketers when they called. He would listen to their spiel and explain why he was not interested or able to take them up on their offer. Most of us just hung up on them, not my brother.

Now there he was, the warrior he had become, ready for battle again. Take no prisoners and show no mercy! The Lone Wolf was at war again! His bravery was stunning and humbling to see. There were so many times I did not think I could love my brother more. Then I would see him go through another obstacle, and my heart would explode with the love I felt for him, explode with the pride I had in him!

He started chemo again that summer. It was three weeks of two-times-a-week treatment. It was very strong and made him very nauseous. But he fought through it. As he kept fighting, his confidence grew, as did ours.

This time around, it was different. We all supported him and talked very often, but somehow we did not feel like he needed us as much this time around. Now we know he did, but he just seemed to have it all under control and knew what he had to do and was going to just do it. The whole situation seemed not as scary, not as desperate. It was; don't get me wrong. But Mark had almost earned a godlike status in our eyes and seemed invincible.

Although he was weak and concerning to see in his condition, I always thought of it as being okay. This was his new body, and he had learned to live with it and had control over it. He was in a lot of pain but managing it the best anyone could be asked to.

In the fall of 2011, Mark had lung surgery to remove what was left of the cancer.

The chemo had shrunk the tumors, so it was a successful treatment to that point. He would have to endure a very invasive surgery, though, and in his condition, that was a large risk. He made it through the surgery with little complications. His recovery was slow, but he fought hard. He had just had more parts of his body removed due to this amazingly cruel disease, but he would not quit.

We were all there for him and the kids. It was a scary time for them especially. They had both thought that this was all in the past and to be a teen still and have to face this again was extremely difficult. They did a great job of taking care of him and the house while he was in the hospital. They made sure the animals were all fed and that Alpine was taken care of too. Whenever we were there to see Mark in the hospital, we would stop by the house and check on them. Alpine was always happy, and the house looked fine. They are good kids with a lot of love for their dad. I could never even begin to imagine what they went through.

The end of the year brought a post-surgery scan that was cancer free!

My beautiful brother Mark had beaten cancer again! Yeah! That's right. The Lone Wolf had won again!

So that meant another victory tattoo for him!

He got an amazing wolf face that was peaceful and stunningly gorgeous. It seemed to perfectly fit how he felt. His spirit was strong even if his body was not. Regaining his strength and muscle mass would be a lifelong struggle. He knew that, but it never got him down.

I watched him struggle with pain and effort every time I had a meal with him. He developed back pain that he dealt with every day as well. My brother probably had more bad days than good, but he never complained. I would call him, and he would tell me that he was not having a good day and that we should talk some other time. But the smile was still in his voice, and he always ended the call with "Love you, hon" no matter how much pain he was in. The respect I was gaining for him was immense.

The year 2012 started with a scan routine back to every six months. All came back clean and cancer free! And then 2013 scans came and went with all clean and cancer-free results. In fact, those two years were health-wise a pretty drama free time for Mark. Of course, there were other dramas in the family, but again, I will leave that for another book.

The year 2013 was also notable for the fact that I bought a house that year. We were very excited to find a house in the Millard area, where I was born and raised. My husband and I had always wanted a dog too, so now that we were not in an apartment, we could get a big dog, just like I had always wanted! Of course, the cat kept us from getting one right away, but we figured she would mellow as she got older. Once we brought home a puppy, she would just have to learn to adjust. But for a time, we would let her just adjust to her new house. Having a basement was blowing her little mind enough for now.

When I think of 2013, I also think of my most favorite Christmas as an adult. Our Christmas that year was very memorable for lots of reasons, all good reasons!

For one, everyone was home! Dan came home from Colorado, and Steve came home from wherever he was living that year. Nashville, I think. He is in construction, remember? So they moved around. That is why it was so special to have everyone under the same roof for a change.

And it was festive indeed! I had gotten Christmas hats for everyone, and we all wore them. We had Santa hats, elf hats, Christmas tree novelty hats, tiaras. It was really fun! We had a big formal dinner and holiday drinks. Everyone was happy and in the holiday spirit! Some of my most cherished pictures are from that night.

We had even gotten a light dusting of Christmas snow!

With what we had fought through as a family, it was very special for us to come together as a family and celebrate the greatest time of year. The love we all had for one another that night is something that I will never forget. We were tolerant and melancholy, and we laughed and teased and hugged and told one another we loved one another by our words and actions. It was as strong as I have ever seen my family together. It was a beautiful way to end the year.

Family Christmas picture, 2013, left to right, back row, Steve,
Dan, Sandy, Laurie and Mark. Front row, Mom and Dad.

The year 2014 started off good.

Mark was as healthy as he had been for a while. The family was
as close as we have ever been, and all was really peaceful.

My brother Dan and his best friend, Ruben, tried to make it
to Grand Island, Nebraska, every year in April for the great sandhill
crane migration. When they could, they would also come to Omaha
and see everyone too. But this year, we had decided to turn it into a
sibling get-together. So with my husband in the back seat and Mark
riding next to me in the front, I drove my car out west. And my sister,
Sandy, and her boyfriend Brian drove his truck. We made the four-
hour trip out to central Nebraska and met up with Dan and Ruben.

It was a blast!

We looked for cranes and partied in the hotel room. We were
loud and laughing too much and just hooting and hollering. We
were rowdy! It was like we were all kids again and blowing off steam.
We went to the visitor center and took pictures of us with our heads

poked through crane wood cutouts. We walked around and learned about them. We drove out to the fields and listened to them and watched them eat. We waited until sunset and watched them all fly out to the river sandbars for the night. The sky went dark with birds …Ha-ha. Sorry. Inside joke!

Wood cutout of crane picture prop near Hastings, Nebraska.
Left to right, Sandy, Laurie, Dan and Mark, 2014.

It was a beautiful day and glorious night!

It was so much fun we promised one another that we would make this yearly trip together. It would be a once-a-year sibling trip that we would take for as long as we were all able to! We laughed about us being grumpy old men and women and complaining about the heat and parking. It was the kind of day you wish would never end!

> *You wished for an endless night, to be able to lasso the moon and stars and pull that rope tight. (Pink lyrics)*

But all good things do come to an end, right? This time Mark climbed in the truck with my sister for the ride back, and we all hugged, said our goodbyes, and hit the road. We all intended to do it all again next year, and we were smiling from our hearts that day!

In July of that year, Mark ended up in the hospital.

He was very weak and unable to get out of bed. He was admitted, and they found he was in a state of malnutrition and exhaustion. He was fighting hard to get stronger, but his body was fighting back. His constant fight with food had depleted his energy and ravished his body. He was still losing weight, and he could not afford to do that. His energy supply was gone. In the hospital, he got fluids and nourishments and rest. He was strong enough to get out after a few days. They performed lots of tests while he was there, and he got a scan as well.

We found out in the beginning of August that the cancer had returned for a third round. This time, it was in his left lung.

I have no words for how we all felt. I will never give cancer that power again. Anyone who has lost or supported a loved one in their cancer fight knows exactly what I mean. Imagine that times three.

The doctor gave Mark one treatment of a double dose "cocktail" of chemo, as he called it. He then wanted to go straight to surgery, as this was the only chemo he would be able to handle. We were waiting for him to improve his health enough so that the doctor felt he could perform surgery. He went in for fluids; he tried his hardest to get stronger. Did he still have fight in him? Yes, to a point.

But as much as I never want to admit it, a part of him was starting to wonder if he could do it this time.

He *never* gave up fighting; please do not ever think that. He was always a fighter, but even the world heavyweight champ will wonder sometimes if he is going to win this fight. In a war for your life, could you win three battles? His spirit never gave up, but would his body be able to support his spirit?

I went to visit my brother today and visited a very thin malnutritional man who just went through his 3rd round of chemo and his 3rd round of another fight for his life. Another

*battle with cancer. Life is very hard & stress-
ful and full on worry is my daily existence.
I ask for some relief from the Universe today
and every day coming up, so I can be strong
for Mark ...again. Who is strong for me? Keep
an eye on me. Also, the earth as there is a
previously undetected meteor heading "very
close" to the earth tonight. Yikes!*

Halloween came and went, and my brother was not strong enough to come over for trick-or-treating, he was not strong enough for surgery yet either.

He came to family functions still, and we visited, of course. But it was getting harder and harder for him to go anywhere. It was getting harder and harder for him, period. It was getting harder and harder for us to see as well.

For the first time, I could relate with what his friend Tony had experienced in his first cancer fight.

It was heartbreaking to see Mark in this condition. Hugging him was a scary thing when I felt how skinny he had become and felt how weak his grip was. He was fading before our eyes, and we could not do a damn thing about it. It was sad and angering at the same time.

Thanksgiving that year was a very difficult thing. We were all so grateful that we were together but somehow could not help but wonder if it would be our last. It was festive, and we had a good time. But there seemed to be this cloud over the table; we all knew what that cloud was.

But we ate our turkey and told stories and pretended it was just another holiday in the old Garaczkowski household. We were very good actors, but we all were starting to see how this scene was going to end. I have to admit, I was a little distant and put-offish that Thanksgiving. Reality was too harsh for me, and I just could not face it. We all looked at one another with sideways glances when we hugged Mark or when he winced in pain.

On Thursday, December 11, I received a phone call at work.

I worked in a big-box store as a manager at the time and was called to the phone on the overhead speaker.

"Laurie, you have a call on line 2. Laurie, line 2."

I picked up the phone, expecting to speak to another store manager or a customer, but it was my mom. She told me that Mark was back in the hospital and I should come up after work or as soon as I could.

She was crying.

Now my mother is one of the strongest people I have ever known. Tears are not shed unnecessarily with her. So I knew it was bad. I went and told my boss I would need to leave as soon as I could. I called my husband and let him know to meet me at home as soon as he could.

The sense of urgency was there. We left within just a couple hours for the hospital.

My nephew Brandon had gone over to pick up Mark for a doctor's appointment and found him on the bathroom floor, unable to get up. Brandon is a big, strong kid, but he did not need to be to pick up Mark and help him to the car.

Of course, Mark's dog, Alpine, had watched over him and kept an eye on Mark before Brandon showed up. He was with him in the bathroom, trying to help. Bernese mountain dogs are bred to help their owners in the mountains; he is a natural hero. He was always the best at assisting Mark getting up and down when he needed it. At ninety pounds, it was not a burden for him. Mark was blessed with a very good, kind dog. He is a special animal for sure and was placed in Mark's life for a reason. I believe that.

Brandon was the one who admitted Mark that day. How hard was that?

He had to make the phone calls that started the relay: his sister Brittany in Missouri, his grandma and grandpa (my mom and dad), Mark's friend Joe. Heartbreaking.

When we got to the hospital, my nephew, Joe and my mom were there. Brittany and her boyfriend had driven back home from where they were living in Missouri and were staying at Mark's house.

My dad was there earlier but had to go home due to his health. I will explain later, but at this point in my father's life, he was on dialysis for his kidneys and struggling with his own health battles. He was eighty years old, not fifty-two, so it's to be expected after a long life to have your own issues to deal with. It would have been more than he could have physically done to be there all day like we were, not to mention the emotional toll it would have taken.

My sister arrived shortly after me. Somehow, we had forgotten to call his friend Tony, and my niece Angie as well. It blows me away even to this day that we forgot, but I fully believe that everything happens for a reason, so I know it happened the way it was supposed to. But it still makes me feel bad that we forgot. It all happened so fast, it seemed.

As soon as we walked into the room, I felt the peace.

We were all wearing masks because he was in ICU technically, but he was not wearing one.

He greeted us with a smile, a tired smile, but it was one of the most beautiful that I have seen on his face ever. He was finally not in pain and in a peaceful state. He looked as good as I had seen him look for years.

It made me realize how much constant pain he had always endured all this time. They had him on pain medicine—very, very strong pain medicine—so he was feeling no pain for the first time in a very long time.

I guess we had all just gotten used to seeing the look of pain he always had. So it was quite amazing to see him like this. Now. At the end.

The staff told us that there really was not anything more they could do but keep him comfortable and pain-free. His body was starting to shut down.

I gasp when I think of those words still.

We were there to watch him die. We were there to send him to Heaven. We were there to say goodbye.

Here is what I remember. Here is what my brain will let me remember at this point.

It is very painful to remember this all, so I will try to type through the tears. Don't get me wrong. There was laughter too.

But above all, there was love.

The family gathered around him in the bed. We all took turns talking to him and saying the things we needed to say. I am forever grateful for that opportunity. I know there are many families and people who don't get that chance. But my brother is a fighter, remember? He was not going quickly and wanted to stay with us as long as he could.

My brother Steve was on his way down from Minnesota, where he was living at the time. It was purely a coincidence and a trip that was already planned—a pure blessing in disguise. Crazy, right? But he would be there by midnight. Dan in Denver would not get a chance to come home. And believe me, it was breaking his heart. He called over and over again, checking on him.

It was late afternoon when the last of us in town arrived.

My brothers' children were trying to stay in the room, but it was difficult for them to watch. Hell, it was difficult for all of us. They were still just teens, and that was their dad. That's a lot to try to wrap your brain around. So they would leave and come back all night. They were there for one another and understandingly wanted some sibling time of their own to try to help one another get through this. I completely get that.

Mark was in and out of it the whole time; he was really fighting. My sister and I stayed next to him, holding his hand, and Mom would kiss him and check on her baby boy. She would try to get him to talk and keep him with us. When he was awake, he was all smiles. He was so happy to have us all around him. We could see it in his eyes. The pure love he felt from us, he projected that love back to us.

We watched *Footloose* and laughed at how cheesy it was with the glitter and '80s hair and fashion. We talked loud and joked as much as we could. To this day, I still have never watched that movie again; not sure I will ever be able to. I hear the song a lot, it seems—in stores, in malls, or on the radio. I finally have gotten to the point where it doesn't break me to hear it. I actually smile and remember the joy in the room that night.

For those brief moments, it all seemed normal. We really were not there to do what we were doing. You could almost fool yourself into thinking that. But then he would become unconscious again, and we would watch every breath he took and wonder if he would wake again. The reality and severity of the situation would slap us all again.

When he did wake up, he would ask, "When will Steve would get here?" He would talk about memories and things that were precious to him. He would want to look into our eyes and told us he loved us more every time we told him we loved him. Those are impressions that will forever be etched in my memory and heart. Those beloved moments are so important. I realize how lucky we were to have them, and none of us took it for granted.

We all got some private time with him. I called Dan in Denver so he could say what he needed to say. We all had our final conversations with him, whether he was conscious or not. But even those conversations in which he could not reply, I know he still heard. We were all doing our best to make this as easy for Mark as we could. He had suffered enough.

When I was sitting beside him once, I told him how proud we all were of our Lone Wolf and how he was such an amazing fighter.

And he howled!

I howled back!

We all howled like wolves because we were his pack. The staff must have thought we were crazy; everyone in his room was howling like a bunch of wild animals!

He told us he had seen Grandma Kosler and she was waiting for him. Was it the drugs, or did she come for him? He seemed lucid when he said it.

The nurse told us that he would more than likely make it through the night. He would slip in and out, but all his vitals remained strong. Fighter. She suggested we all go home and get some rest for the next day. We were reluctant but thought it was good advice. My mom went home to get Dad started on his nightly dialysis, and my sister went home to get some rest and check on her dog, who had been alone all day. We all agreed to meet at the hospital first thing in the morning.

The kids were at home already, getting some sleep, but Joe had decided he would not leave. He could not. He was going to be there for his best friend and did not care about his own health or life. His buddy still needed him. We told him to at least eat something and sleep in the chair in the room if he could. He would try, but he wanted to watch Mark all night.

My husband and I went to McDonald's for something to eat once we were back in our neighborhood. I had not eaten all day and had to get something inside of me. While we were pulling away from the drive-thru, I got a call from Joe. Mark had started to crash again; he was hysterical and told me to hurry.

I told my husband to get back to the hospital. Greg told me to call my mom and my sister and tell them we would be by to pick them up. This is not exactly on the way. Mom is way south, my sister is way north, and the hospital is way east. Greg drove like a madman. He knew we needed to get there as soon as the car could get us there.

I called my mom and sister, and they were waiting in their driveways when we pulled up. I cannot even imagine how hard it was for my dad, not being able to go back to the hospital with us—being alone when your son is struggling to live.

When we got back to the hospital, Joe was waiting. He could not get a hold of the kids but continued to try. Everything happens for a reason …When Mark heard us all back, he struggled to get awake. All his vitals were starting to drop, and his breathing was coming harder and harder. He opened his eyes, saw us all there, and we told him that Steve was still on his way. He was holding on; we could tell.

We all spoke to him again, told him it was okay to leave. He had fought so hard, and he didn't need to anymore. There were lots of words spoken to him. He tried to speak back. I told him that I would get a wolf tattoo for him this time, in honor of him. He smiled and tried to howl.

Greg told him he didn't have to worry about Alpine, that we would give him a home and take good care of him. He smiled very big, and the relief was all over his face. Was that one of the things he was fighting for? One of his worries about leaving this life? It was not anymore. He mouthed "Thank you" and knew in his heart that Alpine would be fine.

My sister had her private words with him, and my mom gave him permission to leave her and Daddy too. I called Dan again and told him we were towards the very end and held the phone to Mark's ear so he could say what he needed to as well.

Then as was the case with Mark, he leveled out again. His vitals rebounded, and he was actually looking better. The fighter until the last breath for sure. He was not ready to go no matter how much we told him it was okay; he still had something to live for.

The nurses again told us that he was steady and that they didn't know how he did it but he was actually looking pretty good again. They didn't know my brother obviously. He had something he was fighting for, but what was it?

Did he need to see Dad again? Was it the kids not being there? At about eleven thirty, my sister, Mom, Greg, and I decided to leave. He really had been improving, and we were positive it was not going to happen on this day. We ran into Steve; his wife, Lyn; and his daughter Stephanie in the hallway, coming up to the room as we left. We were all glad they had made it in time. This would be great for Mark and Steve to have their time.

As we were driving away from the hospital, less than five miles away, I received a text from Joe—Joe, who had never left my brother's side, the best friend you could ask for.

He wrote two words: "He's gone."

I read these words out loud.

I could not believe I was reading it. I could not believe I was saying it.

But my beautiful, strong brother was gone.

It seems he had been waiting for Steve.

As Steve and his family entered the room, Mark opened his eyes, smiled, and after a few minutes, after the words had been spoken that needed to be spoken, he stopped breathing.

He had passed at 11:45 p.m., just fifteen minutes short of the day my Grandpa Kosler had died of cancer. He went to my grandma and to heaven. He was finally at peace and home.

The car was silent except for the sound of crying. I have never felt so much pain from the inside ever in my life. We got to my sister's. Greg drove my mom home, and I stayed at my sister's. She didn't want to alone, and neither did I.

My dad called my cell phone shortly after we arrived, and I had to tell him that Mom was on her way home and that Mark was gone. He was crushed, and we cried together. He made me stay on the phone with him until Mom got home. He didn't want to be alone either.

The rest of that night was full of sobbing and hugs, and we were all brokenhearted. I honestly do not remember going home and going to sleep.

Whenever I woke that night, my pillow was soaked with tears. I was even crying in my sleep. I was exhausted, and the world was gray. It was colorless for a long time after that actually.

I had lost not only my closest brother but one of my best friends. We had watched him for seven years fight for his life, but his body had finally failed him. It was unfair and cruel, the hands he had been dealt. He had dealt with them, though, with more strength and dignity than I could have ever imagined.

My brother Mark, 2011

I would miss my brother every day of my life from then on. You do not get over grief; you learn to live with it.

I had my phone next to the bed that night, and I woke up the next morning to it ringing. It was my brother Steve asking me where I thought we should have the body moved to. Reality was slapping me in the face, and I had not even gotten out of bed yet. The tears started again, and I told Steve to call Brandon and ask him. I was not familiar with mortuaries in Council Bluffs, and Brandon would know.

I threw my phone on the bed and wailed. My body racked with the tears, and I was already asking myself how I was going to get through this.

That was when Mark sent me a sign, letting me know that I would get through it. He was fine, and he would help me.

My phone lay on the bed, nobody touching it, and it started to hit numbers on the keypad. It typed in 7777774444444111111199 999997777777700000009999999 …random numbers in groupings. As my husband and I stared at it, it just kept typing groups of numbers.

"Why is it doing that?" my husband asked. I told him I didn't know.

We looked at each other, and we both had the same thought. It was Mark just telling us he was there. He had crossed over and was at peace. I was sure of it. It finally stopped. I picked up the phone and looked at it. Nothing wrong. Nothing stuck on the keypad.

I hit Clear, and it all went away.

There were many phone calls, and the plans had started. My brother had not left a will and did not even really have a discussion with anyone about what to do with his body when he passed. The only thing I had ever heard from him was our discussion about spreading each other's ashes in the mountains of Colorado when we were both young.

I know that sounds weird and maybe irresponsible, considering he had been fighting with death for many years now. But everyone handles their own mortality differently. There have been some very famous, extremely rich people who have left this earth without a will. I am looking at you, Michael Jackson and Prince. My brother was not rich and did not make plans for whatever reason.

So we were left to wing it, to figure it out ourselves. We had decided where to have the body taken to and had also decided to have a family brunch to discuss it. We had an appointment with the mortuary set up for after that.

At the restaurant, I gave everyone a treasure I had found. I had a bunch of Mark's senior pictures for some reason, and I handed them out. It was a great picture of Mark when he was young—long haired, clear eyed, and handsome. It was an image I had thought was important to keep in our minds as we went through this day, not the cancer-ravaged man that had eventually lost his personal battle.

We had some discussion about what his wants might have been, but nobody had a clear direction. Brandon thought he might have wanted to be cremated; my sister thought he wanted to be buried by Mom and Dad. And every opinion in between. It was going to be a hard decision for sure. But the brunch went well. We had lots of tears, of course, but laughter and good memories too.

Steve, Sandy, Angie, Mom, Brandon, Brittany, and myself met with the mortuary that afternoon, a first for all of us except my mother. When my mom's dad died, he did not have any of his funeral arrangements decided yet either. This caused some serious fighting among the kids. It was not a good thing to have to deal with when you are already grieving and trying to deal with that emotional trip.

My parents had decided right there and then to make all their funeral arrangements for us kids. They had it paid for, and all was decided right down to the outfits they would wear. All we would have to do was pick out readings, music, show up, and grieve. We were extremely lucky children. I told you that already.

A meeting at a funeral home is extremely emotional. It is always still exceedingly raw, and the wound is deepening the entire time. We had to decide what to do, where to do it, and when. Obviously, the first question was burial or cremation. There were lots of conflicting views and opinions, but it came down to a couple things.

If we buried him, where would he be? There was no site next to my parents as they had bought their plots years ago. Did we have a church funeral; if so, where? He was not really going to church anymore, so would his old church let him have a funeral there? Did he want to be buried in Council Bluffs or his hometown of Omaha?

And sadly, it came down to money in some ways too. Burial was thousands of dollars more than cremation. Who would pay for it? The kids did not have that kind of money, and my parents had not planned on burying a child. They were on a fixed budget with my dad's medical care, and issues were piling up too.

But it, of course, came down to what Mark wanted? What were his wishes?

There was a lot of back and forth and forth and back, but it seemed to finally be decided when I spoke a phrase.

"Why would we bury him? Why keep him in this shell? His body had done him no favors in this life, so why make him stay in it forever?" I said. That was really how I felt.

Of course, part of me was also thinking about the promise I had made to him, to spread his ashes in the mountains, and that seemed to me to be all the answer I needed from him. Even if it had been years ago, I really felt this was what he really wanted—to be cremated.

It was then that it was decided. I do not know if everyone agreed with me or if we were all so tired of discussing it, so heartbroken, that we all just decided to agree. It was still an honorable way to go. We would have a small memorial service, but that was the final decision. My brother Steve would help pay for it since he had the most disposable income, and Mark's kids would pay him back with their insurance money. It had been settled.

His actual ashes would not be back in time for the service, so they would provide an urn for display. We all would have the opportunity to buy an urn and receive some of the ashes as well. Mike, the funeral director and owner of the mortuary, gave us a catalog and let us know to call to place the order. Both the kids would want one. I needed one too, again, back of my mind reminding me I needed some to spread. I picked out and ordered a white little mini urn that was called Alpine. I thought this amazingly appropriate, especially since Big Al would be with us now.

We picked out an "In memory" card with a serene mountain stream and a picture of Mark on the inside, with a prayer telling the grieving friends and family that he was Safely Home. The kids would make a picture board, and the girls would order the flowers. The service would be at the funeral home, and we would celebrate my brother's life for the last time.

His fifty-two years, two months, and twenty-seven days of life. Far too short.

An announcement was put into the Omaha and Council Bluffs newspapers with his obituary. The picture we used was a cropped picture of Mark with his two kids when they were little. He had his arms around them both, and the smile was of pure joy and pride. It was one of everyone's favorite pictures of him. We also all posted it on his and our own Facebook pages.

This was on a Friday that we had the meeting with the funeral home and Mike. He was a very nice man and treated us all with a lot of respect, even the kids.

I keep calling them kids, but remember, they were nineteen and twenty-one at the time. But that is still babies in the emotional-experience world.

It is an important job being a funeral director. I have not dealt with many in my life, but Mike was one of the best, I am sure. He actually lived in Millard even though he worked in Council Bluffs; that may explain some of it. (Just kidding, Iowa.) He was very strong and kind, which was exactly what we needed. He treated us all as we were—a grieving mother, heartbroken siblings, and crushed children. I know he does it on a daily basis, and I can't even imagine how difficult it is. I was extremely grateful for his help.

On that Saturday, I called my sister to see if she would come along with me to order the flowers. I didn't even really know where I was going or what I was doing, so I needed her help. She was deep in her own grief and didn't think she would be able to do it. It was just too hard. I tried to convince her, but she was so heartbroken she needed to be alone.

I was upset, but I did understand. We all grieve in our own way, and that was what my sister needed. I knew it was going to be hard. That was why I needed help, but I did not really have anyone else to ask. Everyone else was working or committed.

So I went alone, driving in my car. I was determined to be strong for Mark. I honestly just kind of let my car decide where I was going before I realized I was close to a florist on one of the main streets in Omaha. I pulled in.

I walked in and was asked how I could be helped.

I burst into tears! Holy moly, I had not even started to speak yet.

Obviously, florists work with this situation all the time. I had not even considered this at all and was really embarrassed, but the girl behind the counter just handed me a Kleenex and waited for me to get it together. I was so grateful and actually felt for the first time like I could do this. This bright ray of light behind the counter would help me. When I could, I told her I had lost my brother. Just like that. It was the first time I had said that phrase out loud to a person.

It took my breath away. And here came the waterworks! I would learn that I had to say it a lot in the days, months, and years to come. It never got easier. I can tell you that.

What we had decided at the funeral home was that we would get one bouquet from the siblings and one from the parents.

I told the clerk about my brother and how he was a nature man and loved the outdoors and animals. I had some ideas about what we would want—pine needles, wood, and lilies. We put together an arrangement of white and red lilies, white roses, pine cones, and needle sticks in a birchwood vase holder.

It was perfect!

We did a large one with a white ribbon that said "Son" and a smaller version with a white ribbon that said "Brother." I think my brother would have loved how rustic and awesome they were.

I gave her all the information about where to deliver them, crying pretty much the whole time. She was sweet and empathetic and did not make me feel bad at all. She actually cried with me a few times when she thought about losing her own "pain in the ass," as she put it, brother.

When I walked out of there, I was exhausted not only mentally and physically but emotionally.

How much more can I take? I asked myself. In reality, it had barely even started. I sat in the parking lot for what seemed like forever but was really only about fifteen minutes until I could trust myself to drive. The tears just did not stop. Would they ever? I got home and called my parents to tell them what I had done. I then texted all my brothers and sister and let them know. Everyone was thankful that it was done and excited to see how they would turn out.

I was just pulling myself off the couch and in to get more tissues when the doorbell rang.

I opened the door to see one of my oldest and dearest friends from high school. Sandy G. stood there with a big dish of pasta and a bottle of champagne. I cried and laughed at the same time. As usual, right when I needed someone, Sandy G. was there.

We had always had a strong connection, and I would not be surprised if we were sisters in another life. Our lives seemed to mirror each other at times. She got a divorce around the same time as me. We both lost grandparents around the same time. We changed jobs about the same time and had family members go through very similar challenges in their lives. We would always be friends until the end.

We went upstairs into the kitchen, and I began to tell her what I had done that day at the florist.

"Wait, we need a drink for this," she said.

Truer words have never been spoken. We opened the bottle of champagne and poured ourselves glasses. We toasted my brother, hugged, cried, and laughed. All the stress relievers I needed at that exact moment.

We sat there on my kitchen wood floor, drinking Chandon champagne, crying and talking together. I had a person to tell all my feelings to who was not my family. That was very important to me. I needed to talk about it aloud, and I needed someone who would just listen, someone who really knew me and my family and would laugh and cry with me.

That time on my kitchen floor is precious to me. I do not remember what was said or how long we sat there. But I felt safe and relaxed for the first time since my brother's death. I am sure some of it was the champagne and exhaustion, but it was also the company. I can't imagine a life without my close, true, lifelong friends.

On Sunday, my sister, Greg, and I went over to my brother's to help the kids start to go through things. It was a difficult task, to say the least, but needed to be done. There were so many memories, so many images, so very hard.

While we were there, Joe came over, and we asked him if he wanted anything to remember Mark by. He took some of his favorite memories, and so did Tony when he came by. My husband found a quarter on the floor when we first walked in that was out in the open, but nobody had picked up. He had the strong feeling that Mark had left it for him. He picked it up and cherishes it to this day. Mark tends to leave coins for us all.

I know that they are just things, but they become irreplaceable and very important when their owners are no longer with us and we don't want to let go yet. My sister and I took things that were more personal, family items that needed to stay in the family.

My sister is the holder of all the pictures in the family so she took most of those, that is where a lot of the book images came from. Thanks Sis! I wanted the picture Mark had of my dad when he was baptized. It is in a gorgeous antique frame, and I love the picture of my young daddy.

I also took the vintage Victrola phonograph that he had from my Grandma Garaczkowski. It was a phonograph that my dad had converted into a record player when we were younger. It is made of really beautiful wood and great craftsmanship. I have many fond memories of playing my 45s on that player in the basement when I was little. It looks great in our living room and was too big for my mom and dad or sister to make room for. I am so grateful we have it now.

I took personal things that remind me of my brother. I took a silver ring he had just bought a while back and had showed to me at my parents'. I put it on my middle right hand finger under a jade-and-diamond ring that I bought myself for a birthday and have never taken it off.

I took two T-shirts that still smelled like him—one for Alpine once we took him in to help with the transition and one for me to wear once I could bear to. I took leather and beaded rings he made, also rocks and charms he had collected, a small cedar box to keep them all in, and a dream catcher with a wolf on it. I also took an oil painting of a pheasant that I helped him pick out in Minnesota during one of our vacations. All these items had a special memory and meant something precious to me.

While going through his wallet, I found two things that floored me.

One was a mini card I had given him during his first treatment; it was of a little kitty looking into a mirror and a lion looking back. I had written inside: "This is how we all see you, Mark." It shocked me that he still carried it around in his wallet. I guess even warriors need inspiration sometimes.

The second thing was a picture of me riding a horse when he and I had gone on a vacation in Colorado with our then boyfriend and girlfriend. We were both in our early twenties on this trip, and we would usually meet up with Dan, too, on these occasions.

The crazy thing was, I had a picture of him riding a horse from the very same trip in my wallet too. It touched me and validated that I had a special relationship with my brother and that he valued it as much as I did.

Mark riding horseback on vacation. This is the
picture Laurie carried in her wallet.

On Tuesday, December 16, 2014, we had a memorial to celebrate my beautiful brother Mark William.

He was gone way too early in life but had touched a great deal of people in that short time.

We had our amazing bouquets set up with his picture in a frame and an urn to represent his body. Brittany and Brandon had put together very touching photo boards with some suggestions of some of our favorite images. They spanned his life from his childhood to having his own kids. They really embraced the process of doing these boards, and I feel that this craft project helped in their grieving process. Everyone loved them and laughed and cried at the memories.

There were other bouquets; all guests signed the book and said lovely things. It was one of the hardest nights of my life and one of the proudest. I had total strangers tell me how much my brother meant to them, and I saw for the first time in many years some of his old friends that came to pay their respects to this great man. There was loudness and fun. There were tears and sadness. There was wailing with grief and hollering with amusement.

It was what my brother would have wanted—I really think that.

At one point, I went over and sat with my dad. Due to his health, he was not able to stand for long, and he sat for most of the event. All the guests would come over and sit with him and chat; he was never alone. I sat down next to him and asked him how he was.

"I don't know, El. I never thought I would have to say goodbye to one of you kids."

He had started to cry, and I held his hand and said I felt his pain. I never thought I would be saying goodbye to one of my brothers at this young age. But I admitted to him that I had no idea how he really felt. I had no children, so I don't fully understand that bond. We just held hands for a while.

He eventually said, "This is going to hurt you for a long time, hon. It won't be as bad with your mom and I when we go. It won't hurt as much."

I told him that I didn't think so, that I would be crushed if he or Mom died.

He disagreed again. "It's different when it is your sister or brother."

He had explained that your siblings knew you differently than your parents. You were closer to you brothers and sisters. You were partners in crime as kids. At times they were your only playmate, and you grew up together. You learned about life together. It was just different, he kept insisting.

"But the hardest of it all," he told me, "is losing a child."

I could not give my dad enough hugs that night. He was devastated and would be forever.

I had written something I had wanted to say at the service. Whether I would be able to get up and say it was yet to be determined. But I had it written. It was maybe more therapy than anything, and it felt good to write it. I had always released through writing. I am always more generous at what I can write than what I may be able to say.

My friend Sandy G. had spread the word to my other high school friends about my loss, and they had also seen on Facebook the details of the service. Some of those amazing women were able to come. It was a great surprise and touched me so much. Of course, their intentions were not only with me. Remember, Mark and his friends hung out with me and my friends a lot, so he was their friend too. They had all loved him and would miss him too.

Seeing them all there gave me strength because he did touch a lot of people. And I could see that he still was touching them. So about an hour into the memorial, I had Mike, the funeral director, announce that I wanted to say something. There was no going back now, and I asked Mark for strength to help me get through it all.

As I walked up to the podium, I felt dizzy. An out-of-body experience was happening, and I needed to find the ground again.

I had spoken in front of people before. I was not scared about that. I was scared I would start to cry and not be able to stop, not be able to finish.

Tony, Mark's friend, had walked up there with me; he had come out of nowhere. He talked into the microphone and said "Mark …

dammit, bro, I miss you" and wailed. He cried out in grief then came and stood behind me, crying and holding *me* up. He stood there for a few versus and, at one point, walked away and cried in the back of the room, often wailing with grief and struck by how much he hurt.

My heart hurt with him, but somehow, I found the strength to read what I wrote. All of it. I cried towards the end, but by then there was not a dry eye in the place. I had honored my brother the best way I knew how.

I will not share the whole tribute with you, but here are some excerpts:

> Garzo, Shark, or Lone Wolf—he had many names. He was many things to many people—son, brother, dad, nephew, cousin, boyfriend, BFF, friend, or to me, he was my hero, my big brother.
>
> Growing up, he was always saving or taking in animals in need. He always had multiple animals and still did all his life. Animals have a natural instinct about people, and they all loved Mark. He was one with the animals and nature all his life.
>
> Of course, he still had that German Garaczkowski temper. You didn't see it very often, but when you did, it was serious and for a good reason—usually in defense of someone he loved.
>
> So if you miss Mark and need to know he is still here for us all, look for him in the hawk flying above you, look for him in the woods you walk through, look for him in the howl you hear, look for him all around.
>
> He is the strongest person I have ever known, and I know he will be with me, guiding and supporting me and waiting until we can

touch and hug again. I miss him so much, and I love you more, Mark.

Let's show him that his pack is still here and that we love him and honor him with a pack wolf howl! Hhooooooooowwwllllllllllll!

And with that, the whole room was howling. I still get goose bumps thinking about it. I knew in that moment that I did my brother proud, that a room howling to him was the best gift I could have given him. My brother Steve said to me several times that night, "Are you going to say such nice things at my funeral?" That was when I knew it was a good one. He doesn't give compliments very often, so it was special.

My speech started a couple more moments. Joe got up but was not able to say much of anything until my husband came up, put his arm around him, gave him the strength to put on a "doo rag" (bandana), turned his baseball hat backwards, and said, "Love you, bro." That was the way my brother always looked and wore his hat/bandana. It was all he could do, but it spoke volumes.

My husband got up and read a poem he had written; it was called "Lone Wolf." It was sweet and spoke to all of our love for his spirit. And of course, it ended with a howl. Steve shared some personal stories about his brother as well, ending with a howl again.

My niece Angie also got up and said a few things about her uncle Mark. They had a special relationship, and she had some great and touching memories that she shared. They were proud of each other, and Mark's struggles inspired Angie in some of her own struggles and how to get through them. What she said was beautiful.

The amazing thing was that after everyone got up, we all ended it with another group howl! It was so cool and improvised that it was unreal. Aunts, uncles, kids—everyone was howling! Only at my brothers' final party! He definitely heard us from heaven!

Mark and his kids, Brittany and Brandon.

After that night, I was more lost than I have ever felt in my life. Now what?

Who was I if I was not thinking and worrying about Mark?

I had spent the last seven years watching him fight for his life. For the first time, he was not fighting, and I was not trying to figure out how to help him. I thought *I have to call Mark* so many times in the next few weeks that I was shocked! It had become such a normal day-to-day routine and thought that it was just automatic. Only now, when that automatic thought came to me, so did the tears. So many tears. I became a professional crier. It came out of nowhere and was often uncontrollable. I would hear myself cry out loud before I sometimes even knew I was crying. I fell asleep with tears in my eyes and woke up to a wet pillow full of salt water. It hurt so bad sometimes it was hard to cope.

I was lucky that we had been really busy at work. It was just before Christmas after all. Getting through a shift was relatively easy. I was much too busy to have private thoughts. Although there were a couple songs that would play on the store system that would make me go to the stockroom and wipe some tears away and get myself together before being able to work with customers again.

I also remember one time when I had to tell a customer that was an old friend of Mark's and recognized me as his sister that he had passed away. After exchanging hugs and tears, I had to go up into the office and cry it out.

It was going to be my new reality, and it just hit me. For the rest of my life, I would have to tell people that my brother had died. Would the thought of it always bring me to my knees? Would it always cut so deep every time?

Yes, tears were easy, and I seemed to have an endless supply. Smells did it, seeing hawks everywhere (something that had just started after Mark's death) did it, hearing mourning doves and cardinals did it, but most of all, music. It was the Christmas of Taylor Swift's *1989* CD, and I had received one as a gift. There was one song that spoke to me in particular. It was called "You Are in Love." It crushed me every time and seemed written about the night Mark died and the days that followed. It wasn't, of course. That is just a good songwriter who can create lyrics that speak to so many different people about their own experiences, one that drills into the soul of whoever is listening to it and helps heal or lighten or protect.

I was busy at work, but when I drove home after work, it was hard. The tears started as soon as I got in the car. Nights lying in bed in the dark were hard. The lyrics to that song always ran through my head …

Because I could hear it in the silence of the night. I could hear my tears, hear my brother's voice, hear all the ghosts of what could have been and what should be.

Because I did feel it on the way home. These were difficult drives. All the emotions I had held inside throughout my shift of fake smiles and wishing everyone a happy holiday when I really did not mean it. All the emotions flooded out of me every time. There were times I had to pull over to cry.

Because I could see it with the lights out. Again, the dark. I had visions flashing in my head that I could not control—visions of Mark that last night, of us all in the room. I was trying desperately to hold on to those memories so they would not fade. I was trying to remember every little detail I could, but that was not helping me let go and heal.

Because I was in true love. I held on very tightly to my brother still. I am sure it annoyed him that I was not letting the grief process even start because I was so heartbroken. But he also knew I was doing my best. I was not as strong as him I guess.

> *Taylor Swift's "You're in Love" feels so familiar to my story. Those lyrics, almost every one reminds me of Mark. "You keep his shirt, he keeps his word..." Crazy. It is still the hardest thing I have had to deal with in my life, and I miss my brother dearly on an hourly, daily basis. Trying hard to process it and cope with living still. I need help and self-medicate.*

Later Ed Sheeran had his huge hit "Photograph" that hit the point home with both Mark and me carrying around different yet the same photograph of each other on horses. Many other songs on that CD spoke of all the emotional spaces I was venturing through in a short period. Music is a strong source of healing for me. Pink, I thank you as well, because he does visit me in my sleep.

Life was trying to get back to normal although it never would, of course. There was a part of me that didn't want it to, that if it did, it would somehow dishonor Mark in a way. The world was different now, and I wanted everything and everyone to stop and acknowledge that!

But my life was changing for real.

On December 21, the first day of winter, I went to Mark's to bring Alpine home with me. He had stayed there while Brittany was still in town. But she was leaving now, and it was time for him to come to his new home.

Alpine was very happy to see me and excited for the car ride. He didn't know what was waiting on the other side, but he was always up for an adventure! I got his huge water and food bowls, the couple of toys he had, and his blanket, and I loaded him into my small compact car. He was a sight to see in the front seat for sure.

It was an emotional car ride as I explained to Alpine that he would live with Greg and me now. He smiled his big goofy smile the whole time and cried with excitement, but you know, he's a dog. How much did he understand? He is a very smart dog and polite and as well behaved as they come. But would he understand, or would he wait for Mark to come pick him up? The idea broke my heart.

We got home, and he sniffed the place out. He sniffed the cat out. There was a lot of swatting and running going on by her with the ever-constant hisses too, of course. But they learned to respect each other's space. The cat figured out there are certain places the dog couldn't go, like the bed or couch. So she always had a safe place. Plus, Alpine is the most low-keyed dog and was around different animals at Mark's all his life. A cat was no big deal to him, and he never really gave her a lot of attention after the initial sniff.

So that was that. I was relieved that there was going to be no issues there.

He ran out into his fenced backyard and ran around, peeing on everything, and looked so happy. He had a very small yard at Mark's and was tied up in the front quite a bit toward the end. This spacious yard was exactly what a big dog like him could take advantage of. He was thrilled!

It was an adjustment for everyone but easiest for us. I was so happy to have a piece of Mark—a living, breathing, drooling part of him. Alpine was always happy to see us and gave the best hugs because he was so big and strong.

The first thing we did was give him a bath. Unfortunately, due to Mark's health, he had needed a bath for a while, and we could not afford a groomer. So we put him in the bathtub and washed him down. He fought a little but was pretty good.

If you did not know, Bernese mountain dogs are a breed that has a double coat of fur. That helps them stay out in the cold mountain climate but also makes them not fans of hot weather. This also means that when you wash them, they have twice the fur! There was fur everywhere! It took six towels to dry him off, and yet the under-coat stayed damp. We had to brush him several times, let him dry, then brush again. We had mountains of mountain dog fur!

But he was gorgeous! On his AKC papers, his official name is Garzo's West Rockies Alpine Summit. Alpine was breathtaking! He is such a handsome dog, and when he is freshly bathed, he is so soft and beautiful! It was worth it all.

We also took him to the vet to make sure all his shots were up to date. He was in very good health for a dog who had just turned seven. We did have to treat him for ear mites though. His new vet gave him rave reviews, and our show dog was ready to live his new life.

It doesn't matter how good you look on the outside; sometimes you hurt on the inside. We know that, and we work through it as adults and humans.

Alpine in his new home with Laurie and
Greg in Millard, Nebraska.

How does a dog work through his hurt?

Life with Al was really great. He seemed very happy, and Greg took him for walks almost every other day. We gave him as much love as he could handle, new toys, and treats. He was eating good and loved his yard. He even liked the cat. You could tell when she walked into the room. He would sniff her way and break out his big goofball smile.

But Alpine had his struggles.

He especially had a hard time at night. He would be fast asleep and then jump up and run to the window. He would cry and run from window to window, looking out. He would go downstairs and go to every door, whimpering.

What was he hearing?

Was he dreaming of Mark and still hearing his voice? Was Mark coming to him in his dreams and confusing Alpine?

We would try to reassure him that it was okay, but he would pace around and pant. He was heartbroken and missed his daddy, but how could he let us know besides crying? It was so distressing to see, and it broke my heart. I knew he would adjust in time, but it was so hard to witness.

The next time we took him to the veterinarian, we asked him about this behavior. He said it was likely that Alpine was grieving as well and that it would take him time to learn to live without Mark. It could take up to six months, he had said. All we could do was comfort and reassure him when it happened. Poor Alpine.

My brother never left Alpine at home alone for long unless he was working or in the hospital.

At one point, my father was in the hospital, and I returned from seeing him one night. Alpine had been doing pretty good and had not had an episode for a few weeks at this point. He sniffed me when I got home, and he started to go crazy. He cried and had a basket-case night, looking out windows and pacing around.

I could not figure it out at first, but then I thought about it. I had smelled like a hospital. That made Alpine think of Mark and maybe have some false hope that I had just returned from seeing him. Maybe he thought Mark would come get him soon. I know he loved living with us, but I also knew that he would leave us in a heartbeat if Mark showed up.

Oh yes, he smelled the hospital.

I had once heard a dog's sense of smell put this way: not only does the dog smell your groceries through the bag, but he smells the persons who bagged them, who stocked them on the shelf, and who touched them in the backroom. There are layers to their sense of smell we cannot even imagine.

There were some growing pains, but Alpine eventually learned to love his new home.

We all had to start to learn to live without Mark now.

Christmas came and was, as you can imagine, very difficult. We tried to keep the same traditions, but how can you do that? He had passed away so close to Christmas that we had already bought gifts for him. My parents made most of our gifts, and we each got a big bag full of our goodies and a calendar that spoke of us.

Mark already had his Christmas bag.

He already had a wolf calendar in his bag, along with his home-made goodies.

He was not going to have another year with us though. He was not going to eat his homemade bread or Chex Mix. He was never going to burn the candle I got for him.

When you lose someone so close to the holidays, the memories have already begun. But now, the memories took an unexpected, nasty left turn, and we were all along for this ride.

Christmas at our house was hard too. But we made the best of it and drank our Christmas champagne and toasted my brother at midnight and kissed through the tears.

It was Alpine's first Christmas with us, and we got him his own stocking full of treats. He was so cute that Christmas morning when he watched the cat open her stocking at a respectable distance. He watched her open toys and treats as we fussed over her.

Then it was his turn.

He came over, wagging his tail and smiling in anticipation as we took down his stocking. He loved the attention and treats and new toys. What a great new tradition he was experiencing!

My sister had given him a new toy, too, a beaver toy. It squeaked and had a rope tail and big teeth. He loved it! We called it Justin Beaver, and he played with it constantly! Of course, it shortly lost its tail and teeth and one eye, but that didn't matter to Al. He adored Justin Beaver! He was definitely settling in. It was a beautiful day, and I felt my brother's presence that holiday morning like never before. He approved of the way we were spoiling Alpine, I was sure.

I just missed him so much! It was my first Christmas without him, and it hurt deeply. *Bittersweet* is the word that kept coming to mind.

New Year's was here, and frankly, I was glad to see the year 2014 go! It had been a terrible year and had ended with such final heartbreak that I was not going to miss it at all. I was ready for 2015 to start and looked forward to a fresh year.

We had started to deal with our grief, and as a family, it was difficult. We fought our grief at times, and we fought one another. I have learned it is a different process for everyone. We all deal with loss in the way we feel comfortable and safe. It never goes away, and you have to learn to live with it instead.

I look at our grief like a piece of paper that gets torn. We all tear it up differently. Some of us tear it up in just a couple pieces. They are good tears that can be put back together again with no seams showing. Some of us get torn into lots of little pieces with rough edges, pieces that will never come back together again and be the same. Sometimes we even lose a piece for a time, or we never get a piece back. I was torn to pieces and would be for a very long time.

The new year started, and so began the year of firsts! That is how I looked at the year 2015: the first new year without my brother, the first snow of the year without my brother, the first Super Bowl (when he would otherwise be at my house, watching) without my brother, the first Valentine's without my brother. Every new memory felt tainted and appeared in my mind with an asterisk: *without my brother*.

It has been two months since I had to say goodbye to my brother Mark. It is still very hard and I cry often. There have been several times that the pain is so great I cannot literally breathe. It always reminds me of the Michael Jackson lyrics "Hurts sometimes so bad it's hard to breath." I thought I knew what he meant by that, but I really didn't. Now I do. I miss you, Mark, and feel my loss very deeply. I will take the best care of your boy Alpine that I can. I look forward to the day we get to meet again and touch and hug. I love you so much and miss the shit out of you, my beautiful brother. Fly high until we meet again. Your little sis. XOXOX

It was my first birthday—and it was a big one, fifty years old—without my brother.

Mark and Laurie Christmas 2013

It was especially heartbreaking without my stickers that year.

You see, a very long time ago, my brother Mark gave me some horse stickers in my birthday card. I was a grown adult, but I was thrilled! They were so pretty, and I planned on using them. So thereafter, every birthday, my brother would give me stickers. I would place these stickers everywhere I thought that someone might need a smile, like on the drive-thru at the bank or fast food or the ATM machine. I would place them in bathrooms or in restaurants in odd places. I had many people call or text me and say something like "Hey, I am at Red Lobster, and I see a kitty sticker on the mirror in the bathroom. Was that you?"

I still see stickers I placed all the time, ones that have been there for years. It makes me smile and think of Mark every time.

I got some gifts I would never have gotten if Mark was still alive that year. My brother Dan did send me stickers with my card that year. He was sweet to try to make up for the ones I wouldn't get from Mark, and I love him for that. My niece Angie made a beautiful canvas collage of Mark and some of my favorite pictures (yes, the one of him on the horse is included) that said, "Our beloved Lone Wolf." It is at the end of our hall, and I look at it several times a day. My friend Sandy G. got me a box with a plaque honoring Mark, stating he will always be in my heart. There is a place to put a picture on top, and I put one of me and Mark on our last Christmas together there. I keep all my memories of Mark in that box.

It was a difficult fiftieth birthday for many reasons ...Mark not here, Dad in the hospital. So we didn't celebrate. I feel more anxious than ever. Just waiting for the next shoe to drop ...But it was a pretty decent birthday, a lot of tears and memories. I have hope for the next year of my life, sometimes, when I can find it. I found it briefly today on a walk with Alpine. I saw my first Robin Red Breast!

Spring! A small flock of them actually that Al and I ran through! You got to look for hope wherever you can.

Early in 2015, I kept one promise to my brother that I had made to him in his last hours with us. I had told Mark that I would get his wolf tattoo for him this time. He had gotten two wolf tattoos each time he had beat cancer. This time, I would honor his fight with the tattoo that Mark deserved. This was one of the very last things I had told him as we howled together, and I would do it for him.

The tattoo was a round full moon with a hauntingly beautiful wolf howling in the foreground. Outside the moon were Mark's initials in script, and I had it put on my ankle. It is gorgeous, and I love it! My brother Mark would have loved it too. It makes me think of how he is now and how he howls along with us because he is happy and in pain no more. He is wild and free!

I would get signs from my brother every once in a while—little things that would let me know that he was there with me, that he was still helping and guiding me, that he loved me too, and that we would see each other again.

One of the signs I saw was the TV going off every once in a while. It always came right back on, had just somehow turned itself off. Usually, it's when I was watching something I knew he watched when he was alive as well or when I was watching a show he might have even been at our house watching, like football.

One night at work, I had been having a difficult day and was frustrated and upset when I left. It was pouring out, so I ran to my car and jumped in. When I looked up and out my windshield, there was a quarter on it. It was not sliding down as the water poured down the windshield around it; it stayed in place. I opened the door and got out to get it. As I yanked it off the glass, it was as if it was suctioned on. I really had to get under it and pry it off!

When I got back in the car, I looked at the coin. It was one of those commemorative state quarters, and the state was Kentucky. It had an image of a horse in a stable on it.

I knew my brother had sent it. He was trying to tell me that it was all right, to not sweat the little stuff.

I have gotten many state quarters in strange places since then. I have found Colorado, Minnesota, South Dakota, Iowa—all these places that have meaning in my life. And I found them in the oddest places—in my jeans pocket when I knew I didn't put it there, on the roof of my car, in my bathroom, on the keyboard of the office at work. They seem to come right when I need them the most too.

I have noticed birds behaving oddly around me too.

We have hawks that land on our backyard fence and stare through the window.

We had an eagle flying around above our house on the first Minnesota Vikings game of the year. For the record, Eagles are here in Nebraska but are rarely sighted, especially in the city. My brother often came to our house to watch Husker and Vikings football, so the timing was not lost on me.

There have been so many cardinals coming around that have not been here before. They are always waking us up in the morning, as well as mourning doves. Mark did a perfect impression of mourning doves, and at times, we hear them but cannot find them anywhere, even when we go to where the call came from. They have become little ghost birds.

I once took Alpine for a walk around the lake down the street and had a hawk flying above us and floating like they do on a draft and just staring down at us.

I stopped, and it stopped and just hung there, looking at us.

It was so weird that when we crossed a man and his dog shortly after, he said to me, "What was that all about?"

I asked him what he was talking about, and he said, "That Hawk. He was totally eyeballing you guys. I thought he was sizing up the pet, but your dog is way too big for him to be doing that."

I told him I thought it was weird too. I chuckled as I walked away. It was not just my imagination. That hawk was watching us. Mark was with us on that walk for sure.

In this year of firsts, I admit I really struggled for the first few months. My grief was too strong, and I did not even have the desire to leave the house many, many days. My days off were a blessing, and I called in sick (grieving) on more than one occasion. The idea of having to deal with the world gave me anxiety and a feeling of dread that was hard to overcome.

I cannot even explain how it felt, but I was not really involved in mine or anybody else's life at all. I was checked out. People would talk to me, and I could not even tell you what they had just said. It affected every aspect of my life, and my sadness was all encompassing. I knew nothing else but a heavy heart. Happiness seemed like something I did not remember and would never see again. It was during this time of self-doubt that my dad was admitted into the hospital.

Dad went to the doctor, and they took him to the hospital for tests. He has a blood virus and is struggling with walking. He is strong in mind ...but his body is still failing him. I cannot handle ...I mean I cannot handle losing my dad this year. I ask the universe to watch over him and keep him with us as long as possible. I love him so much and will feel another hole in my heart ...I don't have much left.

On February 9, 2015, my dad fell down at home and was admitted to the hospital.

I lightly touched on this before, but my dad was eighty years old and had had some challenges with his health. I joked with him on occasion, calling him a bit of a fixer-upper. He had a hip replacement, open-heart surgery, and two strokes in the past. He had a pacemaker put in at one point and then was diagnosed with diabetes. It was that disease that did the most damage.

My dad was put on dialysis for his kidney, and by the time he was admitted to the hospital in February, he had been doing this treatment for almost two years. The most recent version was being done at home overnight. My mom had become a bit of a nurse with his illnesses and took great care of him. When he fell on February 9, it started 130 days of moving him from facility to facility and a menagerie of physical events and processes to keep him healthy, alive, and pain-free.

Some of the challenges my father faced were the constant pain, open sores, and weakness in his legs and feet. He'd had a urine infection, bladder infection, and his gall bladder not working properly. My dad went through some very difficult rehab and treatment with hopes of making it back to the house someday. I think we all just wanted him to make it home one more time and be comfortable on his own couch or bed.

I could see the pain he was in every time we visited, and it was hard to see. It was overwhelming to watch another person I loved fight for their life again. I was put in that all-too-familiar role of being brave and positive around my dad, only to melt down the moment I left his room. It was all too much, and I was not even close to being ready to say goodbye to my beloved dad. He was my rock! He always had been, so how was I to go on without that security? It took a physical toll, of course, but mostly mental toll on me.

We learned a lot about the healthcare system for the elderly in those days. Some were definitely better than others. I believe some of his infections were due to the lack of cleanliness in some of these facilities. In fact, my mom got sick from one of them too.

That was an intense day.

My husband and I were visiting my dad, and when we got to the room, my mom was still not there. Well, my mom went to see my dad every day. She was usually there by 10:00 a.m. and stayed until after dinner. She might leave and run errands at times, but she was always by my dad's side. It was noon, and she still was not there.

My dad was a mess!

He is a worrier by nature, something that I inherited from him, so her being late like this was too much for him, not to mention she was not answering the home phone or her cell phone. We would talk to him, and he would not even listen. He would just wait for us to get done talking, then he would say, "Try to call her again." She was his everything and his wife of sixty years. I didn't blame him one bit.

So now I started to worry after a while, and we decided to drive over to see her, make sure everything was okay. Like father, like daughter. I tried to call again as we got closer to the house, and she finally answered her cell phone.

She was in the hospital!

She had gotten very sick and had thrown up and got terrible diarrhea and had ended up being taken to the hospital. We immediately went up and saw her and called my dad's room so he'd know she was okay.

Great! Now both of my parents were in the hospital! What was next?

She had developed a severe gastric infection. She ended up getting out the next day, and we all cleaned up her house for her, as she was still very weak, but I am convinced it came from the facility Dad was in. Luckily, we were able to move him out of there shortly after.

Another thing I learned was, you have to fight for good care sometimes. There were several times we had to get nasty with the staff to get my dad his medicine or food. My mom was on them constantly and took notes of everything they did and gave him.

We assume that they care as much as we do, and that is just not the case. Now I am not saying they were all like that. We did find some very nice rooms for him with some very amazing people. It was more difficult because of his dialysis treatment, because not every place would accommodate that, but it was definitely a learning experience. I am very grateful for the good care we did find.

I am still pissed about some of the bad care we got too. I sometimes drive by one in particular and feel the urge to go in and yell at them still. They caused my dad pain and discomfort he did not need to experience, and I still want to make someone responsible for it! Forever Daddy's Girl trying to protect the man I love!

Dad still in rehab center and in a lot of pain. Mom meets with the doctors tomorrow about his back pain. I hope its late in the day so I can be there. I am pissed about the care Dad is getting and want him back home. Freaking hard-ass times! I just want my dad to get his proper care and not be in pain anymore! They act like they don't know what the hell they are doing!

Every time we visited him, you could see his decline. It was a hard fight for him, and you saw it in his face and motions. As time went by, his body was starting to run down. I often thought of it like a watch. His batteries were slowing down. He was still ticking but maybe not keeping the best time. He wanted to stay with us as long as he could; that you could tell.

At the end of every visit, I would go to his side, and we would have a little one-on-one private time. I would tell him things I didn't share with the whole room, and he would confide in me things about how he felt. I loved those times alone with him because even though there was still people in the room with us, we were alone. The love between us was thick and ours alone.

On June 14, Greg and I went to see Dad as usual.

I had just been to a summer concert with my high school girlfriends the night before and had some good stories to tell him. He enjoyed them all and was thrilled that I had spent time with my girlfriends from way back. My parents always knew how much I cherished these women. We had a lot of laughs and a really fun visit. It was a beautiful day, and we spent some time looking outside at the birds and sunshine.

When it was time to go, I went over to say goodbye to Dad and have our private time. He held my hands and shook his head and said, "I want to go home, El." And I told him, "I know, Dad, but you aren't ready yet. You have to keep working on your rehab and work hard. Then you can be sent home, but you still have a lot of work to do."

He looked at me, shaking his head still, and said, "No, I want to go *home*—not back to the house, but *home*. I am ready to go *home*."

The breath was taken out of me. I stared in shock. Did I just hear that? Did my dad just tell me he was ready to die?

I hugged him and told him I loved him and that I would call him soon and see him next week. I gave him a kiss and held his face so I could look at him and again tell him I loved him.

As I walked out of the room with my mom, I could barely look at her. I knew if I did, she would know immediately there was something wrong. Parents just have that instinct about their kids. There were times I would call my parents, and as soon as I said, hi, they would be like "What's the matter, honey?" And that was it.

It's like that. They know your pain no matter how hard you try to hide it.

As I walked out of the room, I felt my legs begin to shake. As soon as we cleared the room, I grabbed on to my husband and leaned on him for support. He asked me what was wrong, and I told him to just help me get out of there, to get outside.

As we broke through those front doors and into the bright sunshine, I started to weep. Greg, not knowing what was going on, just held me up, asking me what was wrong. I just wanted to get to the car and sit down. Inside the car, I told him what my dad had said. He hugged me and said how sorry he was and that it was okay. My dad was strong, and "He would keep fighting," he said. I was not so sure.

I was crushed to think of what he was going through.

How much pain was he feeling to have those thoughts? How much more did he really have in him? How much could we really expect him to go through? He had his own personal pain and physical challenges that he fought every day. But what about his spiritual strength? What about his emotional limits?

He had told me that there was no greater pain you could go through than to lose a child. Had the loss of my brother been more than he could bear? It was overwhelming and amazingly difficult for me to deal with, but what about my parents? Could you die of a broken heart? I thought you could. I really thought you could.

On Thursday, June 18, I got a phone call at work.

It was a nurse at the hospital. She had called me to tell me that my father had been moved into hospice at the hospital and that I should come right up.

It was about ten in the morning.

It had been 129 days since my dad had fallen and been admitted.

I hung up, ran up to my office, and grabbed my things. I ran into my bosses' office and said, "I have to go. It's my dad." I was crying, and I am not sure what was said to me after that because I had already turned and left the room.

I drove to the hospital at an average of 90 mph. I was so scared I wouldn't get there in time and didn't really care if I got pulled over. Maybe I would get a police escort and get there even quicker!

I called my husband and told him to come up when he could. The urgency in his voice scared me even more.

I was not ready for this! I was not ready to say goodbye to my daddy! How could this be happening? I honestly do not remember the drive.

When I entered the room, I was instantly reminded of that last night with Mark—for obvious reasons, of course, but because of the peace in the room, the peace on my dad's face.

He looked like my daddy, the one without the pain in his face, the one who wasn't fighting for his quality of life. He was asleep and resting comfortably on some very good painkillers. He was pain-free finally. The fight was ending. It was a blessing to see him like that.

We all slowly started showing up until everyone was there except for Steve. He was driving down from St. Paul right away and would be home tonight. And again, unfortunately, Dan in Denver would not be able to make it. He was so heartbroken about it but could not afford a last-minute flight or rental and would have to use those funds and time off for a funeral. What a difficult place to be in for him, and my heart broke for him.

The hospice nurses at the hospital were amazing and would come check on us all the time. They would bring us food and drinks and fuss over my mother and us. They treated us very caringly and helped us all cope with their kind words.

It was looking like it was going to be a long night because slowly, slowly, my dad's organs and functions were shutting down. They turned off his pacemaker, and we all sat and let nature take its natural order. Every once in a while, my dad would wake up and look around the room, as if looking to see who was all there. We told him that Steve was on his way. (Sounds familiar, huh?). He would look around and smile then lay his head back down, close his eyes, and drift off again.

We all took turns holding his hand and kissing him and telling him how much we loved him. He would squeeze our hands sometimes and work his mouth like he wanted to say something.

But mostly I just stared at him. Mostly I just touched him. Mostly I just tried to feel.

I wanted to be there in that moment, and I was so numb still from losing Mark that it was hard sometimes to feel, to feel anything—good or bad. I tried to soak it all in. I tried to knock that wall around my heart down a little so I could embrace it. I will admit it was hard though. My natural instinct was to protect my fragile self. But I could not afford that luxury right now. I *had* to feel it all— the good, the bad, and the drop-you-to-your-knees stuff. This was life, and I could not run away from it when it got crappy. This was the risk of loving someone, and I had decided it was worth it. The room was full of loved ones—my mother, my sister, niece, Mark's son Brandon, my husband, Steve's daughter Stephanie. We were all there and surrounding him with love.

We were also surrounding him with laughter and loud talk and jokes. We were loud and celebrating his life with joy. We were teasing Stephanie about a cute male nurse that kept coming in. It was a family-gathering atmosphere. At one point, a nurse came and closed our door, looking at us like "Don't you people know this is a hospice wing and patients are dying here?"

Of course, we did!

That made the whole room burst out in laughter!

Our dad would want it no other way than to just be us. I am sure he was listening to it all and was proud of his family. Those rowdy Garzos!

Dan would call, and my phone would howl with its wolf howl ringtone that I had been using since we lost Mark. It was his specifically, but I made it my default ring after he passed. We would all laugh because it was like clockwork. We would say, "Dan hasn't called for a while." And just like that, my phone would ring. Or my sister's would ring. He was with us as much as he could be, even five hundred miles away. Even Mark was there in a way, and he was even farther than five hundred miles away!

Finally, the last kid showed up.

Steve had made it back from Minnesota, and now everyone was there. He went to Dad, and we gave him some alone time with him so he could say what he needed to say. He was standing there, touching Dad's head and teasing Dad about the Cardinals, my dad's baseball team, losing their game. Then my dad opened his eyes. He looked right at Steve, and they had their moment. They looked into each other's eyes again. He had made it. He had said goodbye to all his kids, and they got to say goodbye to him.

We visited and waited. Time went so fast that night.

Before we knew it, it had turned into Friday, the nineteenth. Now this had started to make us all nervous. The next day was the twentieth of June. The next day was my sister's birthday. It was already going to be hard enough to lose him so close to her birthday, but to have it happen on her birthday, that was too much.

My sister and my dad's birthdays were only eight days apart and often fell very close to Father's Day too. They had always celebrated their birthdays together, and to have this sad occasion happen during what was usually a very festive, fun time for my family was hard. It was always going to be hard for my sister to really enjoy her birthday again without this negative association involved. But I guess that's part of life—the circle of life to be exact.

We all watched his vitals as they started to descend. His breathing started to slow and get farther apart. We all stood around the bed, watching, crying, saying all the things we needed to, telling him how we felt and that it was okay to leave us. We held hands and hugged one another.

He was a fighter though, and he really tried to be with us all as long as he could. He would force his eyes open to look around and try to reach out or say something. He loved us all very much, and he would miss us as much as we would miss him.

He was really going. Again I was reminded of a clock winding down. Everything slowed; his organs all started to fail. We were assured, and I truly believe, that he felt no pain. He really felt nothing at all, and I was grateful for that thought. After all the pain he was asked to endure, I was relieved it was all over.

A rare image of my Dad smiling in a picture.

He was finally going Home.

At 12:45 a.m. on Friday, June 19, exactly 190 days (or 6 months and 8 days) after saying goodbye to my brother Mark, I said goodbye to my daddy.

I won't relive it all here in this story. I cannot, quite frankly; it's just still too hard.

I loved my dad more than any man on this planet, and I would once again be changed forever with his loss.

But there are two things I must share with you. I mean, you have been along for the ride for this long. You deserve these two amazing stories.

One of them is quite funny and oh so typical of my dad. The other is more of the many amazing things that happened that have got to be a message directly from the other side. Be as skeptical as you want. But it spoke to me then, and it still speaks to me now. I have heard it said, and I believe there is no such thing as coincidence. It is all a universal plan to help us learn our lessons here on earth. I do not believe in black-and-white answers. I believe in all the shades of life and its rhythms.

The first thing that happened was, as we stood around the bed and my dad started to cross over, his breathing slowed. He had been disconnected from the machines, so we only heard his breathing and not the beeps and tones of all the equipment.

We all were silent as it slowed more and more and the period in between each breath was farther and farther apart. The only thing you heard was our crying, our last-minute words to him, and his breathing. It was a very heavy moment and extremely hard and serious. He would breath, and then we would all wait to see if there was one more left. The final breath came, and another did not follow.

He lay still with his eyes slit and his expression peaceful.

We all were feeling all the different emotions you feel at a time like this. None of us moved away from the bed though. We all just stood there next to him. Finally, my brother Steve leaned down and used his fingers to gently close my dad's eyes.

Just then, my dad inhaled! His final breath.

We all jumped!

My brother cleared about two feet in the air as he jumped back so fast! Holy crap! And then we all started to laugh. Inappropriate, I am sure you are saying. But leave it to my dad to have the last word! Steve is closing his eyes, and he was basically saying, "Wait, I am not done yet."

But of course, that was it. That was his final breath, but leave it to him to do something to help lighten the mood! He was still comforting us in our time of need, even from beyond.

The other thing that happened that I want to share was that during those final moments, a nurse had gone to get the clergyman. He was the same priest that had stopped in the room earlier to introduce himself. He had offered last rites at that visit, but my dad had already gotten them earlier.

He came into the room that extremely early Friday morning and joined us around the bed.

We were all holding hands to pray when my sister's cell phone rang.

It was Dan, but this was not the time to pick it up.

When we told the priest who it was, he put a positive spin on it and said, "What a blessing that he called right now while we are praying. He was with us in thought and faith at this exact moment of prayer."

We all agreed. Even if Dan didn't know it yet, he was with us, and we were all connected at that exact moment in time even if we could not all be in the same room. We continued to pray.

A minute later, my phone howled. Dan was calling my phone now, and we all just looked at one another.

We knew it was Dan, but we were thinking of Mark.

We laughed again and explained to the perplexed priest why. My mom told him that we had just lost Mark and that we called him the Lone Wolf. Although we all knew it was Dan, it was Mark who was howling. It was Mark joining us too.

The priest was amazed. He was without words for a few seconds as he looked around the bed at us all. He said, "The Lord really does work in mysterious ways."

Yes, he does.

Then he said, "So now that the whole family is here, let's continue to pray for Jim." Amen!

We all prayed and said our last goodbyes and I-love-yous to this amazing man that was my father. One by one, we walked out of the room and had that final moment with him. I remember it being so hard to leave. Even though he was not there anymore, you could feel his spirit was gone. It was still hard to stop staring at him and embracing my overpowering loss.

The priest later asked us all if he could use that story of the phone calls while we prayed as part of a sermon. He was so moved and amazed at what had happened. His faith told him that the Lord was with us then and the strength of our family brought him to us in the hour of our need. If only he knew …

Then that was it. It was all over. My world had been rocked again, and I had to adjust.

I lost my dad.

I was more than devastated. I was more than heartbroken. I was in a place I had never been before. I was in a club that did not have a lot of members and that nobody wanted to be a part of. I had lost two of the closest people, the most important men, in my life in six short months. I had not even worked through all the grief with my brother's death, and I was now being asked to grieve the loss of my dad.

I could not even wrap my brain around the thought of never being able to talk to him again, never hug him again, never kiss him again, never ask his advice or tell him about my problems again, never laugh and joke with him again, never hear him call me "Elle-Belle" again. He was my first love my entire life, my Daddy, and now he was gone.

We all went home. My brother Steve stayed at my parents' house, so my mom was not alone. She would not be alone during any of it.

I woke up the next morning and tried to face the idea of what was happening. I felt weak and scared and depressed. My pillow had the all-too-familiar wetness of saltwater tears from the night's restless sleep.

I lay in bed, trying to talk myself into getting out of bed, putting one foot on the floor and going from there. I could not. Reality was just too raw and hard right now. I curled up in a ball under the blankets instead.

Would I ever be able to? I had my doubts.

My phone was next to the bed, and it made a sound of notification. I picked it up, but nothing was there.

The phone screen was up though. Then, like I experienced on the day after Mark died, the phone started to punch in numbers: 111 13333666666444444477777766666. I stared at the phone with my mouth open. Was I losing it? Was this really happening?

My husband watched with me, and I said, "Are you seeing this?"

He was. I started to cry.

The comfort I felt at that exact moment was overwhelming. Dad was showing me he had made it. He was okay and at peace on the other side. My brother had even showed him a trick already!

My dad also learned the "Leave coins for me" trick too, as I learned in the time that followed, only his were old pennies, almost always before my birth year or pennies with the shield back instead of the Lincoln Memorial. I always found those ones face down. I saw that as him letting me know he is still protecting me, that he is still my shield.

Seeing those numbers go across the screen that morning, repeating themselves and tapping out somehow happily, it felt playful and came at an exact moment of hopelessness. It shed light in my dark heart, if only briefly. I knew I was not alone and my dad would always still be there when I needed him. Here he was now to prove that to me.

As I got ahold of my tears, I pulled back the sheets and got out of bed. I had to be there for my mom right now. That was what was important to my dad—I was sure of it. His bride and how she would get through was always priority number one for him. I could not let him down.

That day was filled with planning.

We met with the funeral home and finalized the funeral. Remember, my parents had all the arrangements, thankfully, planned and paid for already, so there was not much to do. We picked out prayers for the ceremony, flowers, music, announcements, and prayer cards. All of them were perfect, and we all agreed almost immediately on every decision. It was a stark contrast to making the arrangements for Mark. It was easy in a time that was most difficult.

We all had lunch together and ironed out the details on pall bearers, driving arrangements, and out-of-towners' accommodations. Dan was due in soon as well as Mark's daughter Brittany and her boyfriend. They had decided to leave their son home. He had enough death in his short little life already. Dan would stay with my mom, then Steve would go home to pick up his wife, and they would stay in a hotel nearby. It was decided that Brittany and William would stay with me and my husband. Brittany was excited to see Alpine again! We were all coming together as a family, and I knew my dad was proud of us.

The next few days were a blur of emotions and activity.

I bought a dress for the ceremony, crying my way through Kohl's. The dress I picked, though, I saw right away. It was black and blue (my dad's favorite color) with a floral print. It fit perfectly and was on sale. Done.

We all stayed busy with communications and arrangements. Then the day came to lay my dad to rest.

He looked strong and handsome in his casket. It is funny that you often hear that someone "looks good" when they are dead. But that was exactly how he looked.

The viewing was the night before the funeral and was busy and loud with memories and stories and laughter. At one point, I went up to my dad in the casket and told him I knew he was there and enjoying himself. The sound of his friends and family were exactly what he would have been thrilled to be a part of. We saw some good friends and relatives that we had not seen for a while come to pay their respects to my father. All of my aunts and uncles, cousins, and my dad's nieces and nephews were there. My dad was very loved and respected, and I was very proud.

My father's funeral was beautiful.

The flowers were blue and white on his casket, and the ceremony was gorgeous. There were many flower arrangements scenting the church with nature. There was much pomp and circumstance as there should be. The prayers were sung by the priest, and the readings were perfect. They really knew my dad, and they loved him too.

My niece Angie somehow found the strength to get up and say some really beautiful words about her grandpa. It was touching to us all and moved the entire church. I was impressed and proud of her for finding the strength to honor her grandpa this way. She once again surprised me with her courage.

The drive to the cemetery was down streets that meant a lot to my family—our old stomping grounds and places that held many memories of the good times in the past. The funeral director made it as special as possible. I remember feeling so important and exceptional, almost royal, as they blocked traffic and let my dad through, followed by the people who loved him. It was a very remarkable last drive for this special man.

He was buried next to a tall sturdy tree and with a great view for when we visited him. They were difficult, bittersweet moments, ones I will never forget: the last time I saw my dad, the last time I kissed his cheek, the last "I love you" until we meet again. It was all almost impossible for me to grasp. I really had a hard time believing it was happening at times. But the memory that made me rush back to reality was sitting next to the casket, praying, before they lowered it and taking some of the blue carnations as I numbly left.

It happened, and now it was over. It happened, and now it all started.

I sat on a sunken dock today that I had to walk through the lake to get to so I could get to a dry area to sit down. I sat with my legs in the lake, surrounded by water—literally sitting on the lake. And I thought that it was the perfect metaphor for how I feel right now ...surrounded and inches away from drowning. Anxious and nervous is how I feel always! The beauty of the lake rippling in the late-day summer sun somehow pierced my heart for what has been, what is, and what will and will not be. I am desperate for relief and moments of relaxing for real and for peace of mind! I ask that of the universe right now.

A couple weeks after my dad's funeral, I got a tattoo on my wrist. It says "Roy James" in script writing, and below in, my handwriting, it says "Dad" in blue with a tiny red heart. I had told him I was going to do it after I got my wolf tattoo for Mark. I told him I wanted his name on my wrist. He said that was a nice gesture but that I shouldn't do it for him. He wasn't crazy about tattoos, but it's what I wanted. I may get more too.

One reason I got it was, of course, to honor him and to be reminded of his proper name every time I looked at my wrist and also, I think, to show other people, complete strangers, that I once had a dad that I loved, that there had been a man named Roy James that had my heart. I also wanted to feel the tattoo. There was a part of me that wanted to feel the pain. I was mentally and emotionally in pain from all my recent loss. I may as well be in actual physical pain.

With Mark's tattoo pain, I thought of all he went through and all the pain he endured. I certainly could handle a little needle. With my dad's tattoo, I thought of all the pain and sadness I had felt and how unfair my life, in my mind, had become and how I deserved and expected the pain of this tattoo. The more it hurt, the better. I was angry at life when I got this tattoo.

There are, according to experts, stages of grief. The stages are denial, anger, bargaining, depression, and acceptance.

Denial

This is one I never really embraced. There was no denying what was happening in my life during this period. I often said, "This can't be happening," but it was said with the knowledge that, yes, in fact, it was happening. All my denial seems to come before anyone died. I refused to believe I would lose my beloved family members.

I was in denial at times about how bad it really was with both my brother and my dad. But after they died, and I was fully in grief, there was no denial. I could not deny the pain or loss I felt. I could taste it and smell it at times; it was so tangible. It would often take my breath away; it was so real. I could not deny that my new reality now had two less people that I loved in it. I did not want to, but I believed it. I knew it was true—horrible and heartbreaking, but true. There was no denying that.

Anger

This is one that I did embrace. I still take it out and play with it from time to time. It is all kinds of wrong, and I know that. Even in the moment that I am at my most angry, I know it. But I cannot stop it, nor can I stop myself. It is a form of release from all these deep cuts and hurt I have.

Is it a healthy release?

No, not really.

But I am still very angry with the universe and what it has taken from me and my family, and sometimes I need to let the universe know that. It is unfair and cruel, and I am mad about the hole it has left in my life and heart. I scream and yell and throw things and say nasty things I don't mean because I want somebody else to hurt like I do. I want somebody else to feel bad with me.

I remember one specific time that I was angry and lashed out. I had ordered a bacon cheeseburger through a fast-food drive-thru, and they had forgotten my bacon.

I lost it!

I drove back through and yelled down the drive-thru attendant and berated her for her inaccuracy and asked her what was so damn difficult about the job that she could not figure out. How dare she screw up my order! I demanded to see a manager. I then proceeded to yell him down for not hiring and training his staff properly. I was unreasonable and did not accept anyone's apology.

It was not the bacon. That was grief. That was all it took for it to come show its nasty face again.

I drove away, crying so hard, and was disappointed in myself and the way I had treated them. I felt incredibly bad and embarrassed. But there it was. There was my heartache coming out in any way it could. I am not proud of some of the things I have done in my weak moments. But I always try to identify and learn from them.

My dad had told me when I was little that I can make as many mistakes in my life that I need to as long as I learn something from each one. I have learned a lot from anger.

Bargaining

Although I knew it was impossible and not real in any way that I believed in. I did ask favors. I did ask God to help my family members with their struggles. I did make promises in return.

Is that bargaining?

I begged for mercy and help in understanding why this was all happening, and I would be merciful to others if I could just understand. Do I call that making a bargain? I told the universe that if they would help my dad make it to the sixtieth wedding anniversary, I would do random acts of kindness every week. Was that bargaining?

I understand the concept of saying if you would just do this, I will do that. But when dealing with grief and the process of losing a loved one, does anybody really think that making a deal, so to speak, will help save their loved one?

Yes. I have seen it. Well, maybe I have. I believe I have.

When my father had open-heart surgery, my mother told God that if he would just let my dad get through the surgery and heal, she would go to church every week, twice a week. Well, my dad went through his surgery, and my mom went to church every week, twice a week, for a very long time. My thoughts on this were that she has amazing faith and loyalty to that faith. She asked, she received, and she followed through. I do not know very many people who have that kind of faith and loyalty to their own words.

Some may call it foolishness. I don't know about that. But my dad came through a very high-risk quintuple open-heart surgery with complications. He had his heart stop several times on that table but kept coming back. So who is the fool?

Depression

Hello, darkness, my old friend.

When my brother died, I went to a dark place. I had a hard time learning to live with my loss and thought it was something that I was totally alone with. Nobody could really understand what I was going through, or so I thought.

They would talk about losing a grandparent or distant relative, and I would just stare at them.

Were they kidding? How can you even compare the two?

Did you grow up every day of your life with your grandpa? Did you get grounded with your great-aunt? Did you have secrets with your grandma that only you two knew about? It just was not the same.

Once my dad died, it was magnified even more how very little anybody understood how I felt and how it was consuming me. I would tell someone of my two losses in such a short time, and they wouldn't know what to say. It made them uncomfortable.

The only people I found who really understood were my family. I spoke often to my sister and brother Dan about how we were getting through. We had good days and bad days and would reach out and share the sadness and feelings of pain.

Grief is funny that way. You can be going along, having a perfectly normal day, and then bam! You smell something or hear something that drives it all back into your gut. It is there again and fresh and raw, and the tears come again. One thing I have learned about the loss of someone you love is that you want to talk about them. There is so much power in the stories and memories and just saying their names. This often alleviated my depression, if only for a short time.

I mentioned it before, but I truly checked out of life during this time. I would go to work and not care about what the tasks for the day were, what the meeting was about, what anyone was even telling me to do. I was on antianxiety medication at this time because I had issues just dealing with life. I really did not care about anything anymore. I was working hard at not slipping into depression, and it was a daily battle. I fought some demons during this time. I was unhappy in my job, unhappy in my health, and unhappy in my life. Changes had to be made.

Acceptance

I have been dancing with acceptance. I mean, I accept that I have lost my dad. I accept that I have lost my brother. I accept that I will never see either one of them again in this lifetime. I accept that my world is different.

You never ever get over losing someone you love. You never get over missing them. What you do is learn to live with that loss. You don't forget the loss. You relearn how to live without them. You adjust your heart to accept the fact that you will not touch or hug them again. You train your memory to hold on to that last kiss and the sound of their voice. You start to accept it, slowly in my case, because I just miss them so very much. But what choice do I have? It is what I have to do—accept it.

And I feel, most importantly, you look for signs from your loved ones to let you know that they are there with you. They are there when you need them, and they miss you too.

They show you signs in different ways. They sometimes are subtle, and they are sometimes not. I believe these signs are their ways of helping us adjust to life without them. They are sending little hugs to help us heal. They are sending messages so we know they are still with us and hear us talk to them.

I have mentioned a couple of signs that I have received from my dad and brother—the coins and the phone acting up. But there have been many more. All of my family have seen them. My sister will see feathers and rainbows. My mom has a cardinal that comes and visits her every morning. Somebody wakes me up at four in the morning very often, always at exactly 4:00 a.m. in the morning.

How do I know they are signs from my dad or brother? you may ask. A rule of mine is, if you find something where it shouldn't be—a feather, a coin, a number—that keeps repeating in different places and that object or abnormality makes you think of a loved one, it was probably sent from them.

I don't believe in coincidences, remember?

Chapter 4
The Flavor

You are not a human being having a spiritual experience; you are a spiritual being having a human experience.

—*Pierre Teilhard de Chardin*

This is the part of the story that gives you condiments for your sandwich.

Condiment as defined in the dictionary as "something that gives a special flavor to food."

This is your lettuce, pickle, and tomato part of the story.

This is the onions that will bring you to tears, but you just can't help yourself. This is the cheesy part of the sandwich that just makes you smile when you taste it. You don't need this part to hold your sandwich together like the spread. This is the part you need to enjoy your cravings of deliciousness and to feel satisfied, the part of the sandwich that is the ultimate reward to all the work you have put in, deciding what to enjoy for your body fuel, your reward for reading about the highs and lows of some good people. You have come along with me for that ride, and this will be how I hope to pay you back.

Remember, the body does need food for fuel, but it also needs positive energy.

And it needs healing time when hurt. And its needs strength, mentally, physically, and spiritually. And it needs faith and hope.

And most of all, it needs love.

As I have alluded to in the previous chapter, I was not in a good place. After my dad died, I had real coping issues. I lingered on the edge of depression and was very difficult to be around. I had a dark heart, and I wore it on my sleeve.

I asked for help a lot—not from the people around me, but from the heavens. I asked for mercy from God, Jesus, and all the angels. I needed help from the universe and all my loved ones who were still with me. I prayed to my brother and father almost constantly to help me find peace.

I was unhappy with my job and the people I worked with. Everything there changed after my dad died, and I was seen as a weak person, I suspect, because I was grief-stricken. No blame to them, though, because how could they possibly understand how I felt? I hated that they drove us so hard and rewarded us so little. I was disgusted by the whole corporate mentality of moving up the ladder and having power.

All those things I cared about before meant nothing to me now. How could they? It seemed so unimportant in the grand scheme of life and how precious and short it had seemed at that time.

One thing that did happen right after my dad's death that helped to renew my faith in the world was a phone call I received.

A few days after my dad's funeral, I got a call from the man who owned the mortuary that buried my brother. Mike called me after seeing my father's announcement in the paper to offer his condolences. He was very kind and expressed how very sorry he was, saying, "No family should have to go through something like this."

Finally! Someone who really did understand. It was his business to understand in fact. He asked about my mother and how she was doing. He asked about the rest of the family.

Then he reminded me that I still had not picked up the ashes of my brother's that I had ordered. I had ordered a small urn with his ashes right after he died and had received several messages from them, telling me I could pick it up. I had just never had the chance to do it yet. With everything going on with my dad, I had never found the time. And of course, I had needed them someday if I were to spread his ashes in the mountains, as I promised.

I apologized to Mike for not picking them up yet. He said he had not brought it up because of that. He brought it up because he was going to drop the urn off at my house for me. "You need your brother with you right now" was what he had said.

I broke out crying. I was so deeply touched by this kind gesture that I had to sit down because my knees went weak. When I could speak again, I asked how much I still owed him for it so I could have it ready. He told me that he was going to cover it for me, to not worry about anything right now but healing my heart and taking care of my mom.

An angel answered some of my prayers that day, and his name was Mike. I will forever be grateful to that moment because that was the first moment that led to the rest of my story.

In August, on a Sunday, I got a phone call from the manager of a store that I had been trying to work at for a very long time. They wanted to set up a job interview. Who gets a phone call on a Sunday about a job interview? I was so excited! It was a store that I frequented quite regularly, and I used all of their products. The idea of working there was perfect. I had the interview two days later and got an offer that day. I was so happy!

I could give my notice and leave the job that was making me miserable and move into what surely had to be a better environment. I did, and it was.

I went to my dad's grave site the day after I got the offer. As I told him about getting my new job, I clearly heard my Dad say, "Good for You Elle". Clear as day. Like he was sitting right next to me. A breeze blew right then, and I got goose bumps. I laughed at the hug he was giving me. He was there. I was sure of it. As tears rolled down my face, I knew, I knew my dad had a little something to do with my job change. Thanks, Dad!

As I said, I do not really believe in coincidence. I believe everything happens for a reason and that people are brought into your life for very specific reasons.

My whole thought on the job I had while my brother and dad passed over is this. I left a job as a buyer to work there, and in that previous position, I traveled a lot in that career and would have more than likely been out of town during my brother's passing. Even during the days my dad was going through his battle, I would not have been home enough.

So even though I only worked at this job just around a year, it was good timing. It gave me the luxury of being able to be home during this period. It also gave me the ability to leave my job both times I needed to in those final moments. The job I currently have would not have given me that freedom. We often run on a small crew, and I could not have just left the store. The job I had during those difficult times had a large staff and was a big-box store that was never run by only one person. I could always leave in times of emergency. I am so glad it all happened the way it did. It was all part of a bigger plan to help me through this devastating time of my life.

Ever since Mike had brought over the urn full of ashes, I had felt a hundred-pound wolf on my back. The promise I made to Mark was real and constantly in my mind as something that I *had* to do. I thought about it all and how I would do it. It was overwhelming to think of, but I had to even though I was still struggling to find my strength and my peace of mind. I had this responsibility that I took very seriously.

At this point in my life, I was fuller of insecurity and anguish than I had ever been. Situations in my life had changed for the better in some cases in what felt like the first time for a very long time. I hesitantly embraced the positive, but I always had the feeling that the rug would be pulled out from under me again if I let my defenses down though.

A feeling of dread was always there, a constant anxiety that was flipping my stomach over and over. How could I escape it? I could not live like this for much longer. I was drowning, and I could not breathe.

It was time for me to run away from home. I finally decided it was time for me to fulfill my obligation and to try to heal myself at the same time. I had this grand illusion that if I went to the mountains to spread Mark's ashes, it would also spread my grief to the earth too. My mountains have always been the answer in my times of need. They always healed my soul when I needed it the most. It had to be the answer.

But how could I do this?

How did I think that I was even close to being able to do such a strong thing as climb a mountain and spread ashes to the earth to honor my brother? Just the heaviness of those actions made me cringe with fear.

The woman I used to be could do it. The woman I was before grief clinched its fist around me could do it. But for the first time in my life, I was scared to try. I consider myself pretty brave. I always thought of myself as someone who had courage. I went to the mountains alone and hiked in nature alone for gosh sakes. I loved being alone in the middle of nowhere. I loved the vastness of the land and how little it made me feel.

The thought of doing this was terrifying to me now. I found every excuse I could think of not to do it because here is the thing—I knew I had to do it alone.

I knew it. I am not sure how I knew it, but I did.

When I thought of the logistics of doing the actual spreading of his ashes, I always thought of it as something I alone had to do. I never really questioned why I thought that, why I knew it. I just did. Would I be strong enough though?

As I said, the excuses had started though.

I did not have the money to do this. I did not have time off from my new job to be able to do this, and I certainly could not ask for time off already.

It was almost September in the Rockies. That meant aspen leaves were turning and that people were coming to see them. I would never find a room, and if I did, it would be expensive during this time of year.

I had every excuse ready as an answer, ready for the questions I was asking myself inside. The part of me that was pushing for it to happen, the part that knew it was actually exactly what I needed—if I could only find the courage to listen to myself.

So the end of August answered a couple of the questions for me.

I got my final check of the month, and there was a $257 bonus on it. I had not expected it, and even the store manager was not expecting it. It was an "event" bonus from an incentive that had just kicked in. Interesting. Well, there was the money I needed. Okay, well, I still needed the time off to go, and I did not feel comfortable about asking for it.

Then the first few weeks of the September work schedule got posted. Somehow, I had ended up with September 11–16 off. What? It was from some paid days off I needed to start to use before the holiday season started so I would not lose them. I had not asked for those days off. They just happened, and I would get paid for them.

Crazy, right? But here is the really crazy thing. Mark's birthday was smack in the middle of those dates. Mark's birthday was September 14. I could actually go spread his ashes on his birthday. The universe was brilliant!

I had not even thought to plan it out that way, but here it was. I was being pushed to do it and to do it on a very significant day. All the messages and signs were there.

I denied them still because I was still scared. But when the universe and God has plans for you, you can't run away or deny them when they slap you in the face like I had just been slapped. I had a little part of me starting to believe it was going to happen and that I could make it happen. A part of me knew this was exactly what Mark wanted and that he was going to help me every bit of the way so that it would happen. That part of me just needed to be nurtured so it could grow. The spark needed to be fanned to a flame.

After many discussions with my husband, who was very encouraging, I decided to start to plan for this trip to the mountains. I next needed a place to stay in Estes Park. I told myself that if I could not find a place at a reasonable rate or even a place at all, it was not meant to be. I gave the power again to the universe and let it decide my fate. I called the place that I stayed at when my husband and I took our trips out there. They needed a five-night commitment to stay there, and I was only staying four nights. Strike 1.

I called the place I used to stay in when I did my solo trips, and they were booked for those nights. Strike 2.

I called another place that a friend of mine always stayed in and I had always wanted to stay in. They had no availabilities for those nights. Strike 3.

I was done. I was ready to throw in the towel and give up. I had tried, and it just was not working out. I had made an agreement with myself that I was placing it in fate's hands, and maybe it just was not meant to be. Maybe I just was not ready yet.

A voice in my head kept nudging me and telling me, "Try Castle Mountain Lodge." This was the place that we had stayed as a family the last time we all went out there. I had resisted calling them because it just seemed like that place would be too hard to stay in. There were so many memories of being there with Mark and Dad and the whole family. It was an intimidating thought. Unable to stop the voice in my head, I decided to throw caution to the wind and give them a call. This was the final try, and then I had to let it go.

I called Castle Mountain Lodge and asked if they had any rooms for those dates.

The lady at the desk said, "Well, the traveling gods must be with you. We just had a cancellation less than an hour ago."

Well, surely it won't be a room I could afford. She then told me that it was a streamside room with a fireplace and two beds. It normally went for $179 a night, but because I was staying four nights and she didn't have anyone else to take it in such short notice, she gave it to me for the single-occupancy rate of $79 a night. That came to $316. Because of my unexpected bonus, that meant I only had to come up with $59.

Here we go again. I believe that room was mine and was saved for me. The traveling gods indeed …or something like that.

So it was settled. I was going to the mountains to spread Mark's ashes. I would also take something of my dad's to help set his soul free with Mark's. The serious planning had begun. I kept it very private. The only ones who knew what I was doing were my husband, Greg, and my mom.

As I said, I do not know why, but I instinctively knew that I had to go alone. It was my burden to bear, and it had to be mine alone. If I was to honor my brother and dad, I had to do it the way I knew they would want it done. If I started to bring others in on it, it would alter. There would be different opinions on where and how. It would diminish the importance of the event in my mind.

Plus, let's face it—I needed to do this for myself too. I had to do this to heal and have my soul scrubbed clean again. I do not call it closure because the wound and pain will always be with me. I never get to close the door on the grief, and I do not think I would want to if given the chance. Missing and loving my brother Mark and my Dad was who I was now. I had to start to see that and look for the silver that was lining those dark clouds.

The first thing I needed to do was prepare for the "ceremony." That was how my mind started to think of it—to get those pieces of my loved ones together so I could set them free on a mountaintop.

I knew exactly where I would do it too: Lake Haiyaha! Of course!

It had some of the greatest memories we have as adults of sibling love that any of us can remember. We all still talk about that day with warm hearts and colorful memories. It was perfect!

It was decided. I would drive out on the eleventh, spend the twelfth and thirteenth acclimating to the altitude before doing the hike up to the mountain lake on the fourteenth—on my brother Mark's birthday. It was perfect and seemed meant to be. There was no going back now.

I thought long and hard about the actual spreading and what would actually be spread. I got little ziplock baggies that come with my hair color kit; it measures about two inches by three inches, and I used those for both my brother and my dad.

The one for my brother Mark had some of his ashes obviously, plus some of Alpine's hair that I cut off his chest and head, telling him they were for his daddy. He had some of Alpine's heart and mind with him then. On the outside of the clear baggie, I used some Sharpies to write, "Mark, our beloved Lone Wolf and warrior survivor! Miss you and love you more, Mark! RIP always." And I drew a wolf howling and hearts all over it.

In my father's baggie, I put a very small picture of him that the church had taken for my parents' sixtieth wedding anniversary announcement. Somehow, I had ended up with the mini proofs when given my copies of the photos. (Hello, Fate.) It was a handsome picture of him. He was actually kind of smiling, which was rare for my dad. It was about the size of my thumbnail. I also put in some confetti from the sixtieth wedding anniversary party that I had kept. They were little pieces that looked like hearts and white doves and diamonds. The sixtieth wedding anniversary is the diamond anniversary after all. On my dad's baggie, I wrote, "RIP, Dad! Our hero. We will miss you and love you always! XOXO." And I drew hearts and a rainbow on it.

I then put both of those baggies in a velvet drawstring bag and put them with my hiking gear. Although the velvet bag was less than a half pound, it would be the heaviest thing I carry on that hike.

Now that the plan had been set in motion, there was an undeniable weight on my soul. I cannot even explain how it felt, but the seriousness of it and the fact that it was being kept a secret was like a huge monster under my bed. It was scary. Most of the fear was in my head, but there was also a real possibility it was right there under the bed too. There was a very real possibility that I could do this hike alone and spread the ashes properly and return without a single regret, but there was also the chance that the hike would be the monster I could not conquer.

And if I did it all and returned and told the rest of my family what I did without them, then what? Is that the moment when the monster would slash my heart open?

After all, my brother Dan's birthday is on the twelfth of September. I would be in Estes Park on that day, only a seventy-mile drive from him. The guilt I felt about not telling him I would be there, not giving us the chance to hang out for his birthday, was a taste I could not get out of my mouth. It was a very bitter taste and was like acid reflux the way it kept coming back up to my taste buds. Would he forgive me? Would the rest of my family be mad I did not include them? My insecurity over this issue was huge, but again, I had to listen to my gut and what it was telling me to do. And the gut said to do it alone. My heart said to do it alone …and eventually my mind agreed.

To say I was very fragile at this time in my life would be a gigantic understatement.

I was fragile in my emotional, mental, and physical health. *Emotional* and *mental* should be obvious to you by now. The physical came from not being able to eat, my nerves being shot, anxiety off the charts—all those symptoms you would guess someone going through a deep loss of two loved ones would have. I had them all.

With an extreme heaviness and seriousness, I packed for Colorado. I packed the usual way, bringing my dry goods and trail food, packing all my different layers of clothing to be ready for any kind of mountain weather. I brought shorts, T-shirts, sweatshirts, long pants, coats, hiking boots, and my hiking gear, including my velvet bag containing my loved ones.

But unlike any other time in my life packing for a mountain trip, there was not a lot of joy in it. It even felt like work to a point, a mission I was preparing for, one more battle to prepare for in my personal grief war. Inside I actually thought it would be my last battle, that this would be what I needed to move on from my heartache and sadness. This would be the end game.

Silly girl.

Fragile as I was, I had a couple of dreams that I clung to when I needed strength.

The first one was a dream I had about my brother Mark. In my dream, I had walked up a rainbow that was like a stairway into the clouds, and when I got above them, I was in a room. The room was all white in every direction, but when I looked up, there was outer space. It was dark as any sky I had ever seen and filled with more stars than I had ever seen in my life. And the stars were bright and colorful.

Then I looked around the room in every direction and saw nobody but my brother. Mark was standing off to the side, and he was holding a sign. It was a handmade sign made of poster board. And written on it were big letters made of poster paint: "YOU ARE …" and another word. The last word on the bottom was telling me what I was; I could just not quite make it out. It was like it shifted shape and changed letters, but I could tell you this. It was positive. Whatever Mark was telling me, it was good. He was smiling and jumping up and down with this sign and was very excited for me to see it. I *was*! The memory of it still makes me smile.

The other dream involved my dad. He was lying in his hospital bed and looking weak and sick like I had seen him so many times before. It started in that way, and it hurt my heart to see him like this, just like it always had. But then I sat on his bed, and he sat up and looked me right in the eyes, nose to nose. He had amazing, beautiful blue eyes. I got my father's eyes, and it has always been one of my most attractive features.

As he looked deep into my eyes, he reached down and grabbed my hands. He wrapped his fingers in mine, and he told me I was strong as he squeezed my hands. He said, "You are much stronger than I am, Elle. You are." And I cried and told him I missed him and I was not stronger than he was. He laughed and squeezed my hands and said he loved me too and that everything was going to be okay and that I needed to remember how strong I was. I woke up from this dream and felt the tears on my pillowcase, and my fingers still ached from him squeezing them.

I carry both of these dreams as a source of strength and as clear messages from my brother and dad that they do know what is going on with us after they leave. They know what we need to get through those hard times and celebrate with us in the happy times. They believed in me. They came to me in my dreams and encouraged me and filled my heart with the support and approval that I needed from them.

I leaned on these dreams as a crutch many times. I used it as my walking stick throughout my whole trip to the mountains.

I came across this quote shortly after my dad's dream; I repeat it in my head when I have self-doubts and fears. I think he would have loved it!

> *On the darkest days when I feel inadequate, unloved, and unworthy, I remember whose daughter I am, and I straighten my crown!"*
> —Unknown

Here it was September 11, 2015.

Not even three months after losing my father, but it was time to straighten my crown and get on with it.

What a day to start a trip like this. Patriots Day.

I was thirty-six years old on September 11, 2001. Any one of certain ages who lived through that day remembers what it was like. It was a life changer, and everyone has a story on where they were on that day and how it affected them—not only 9/11, but the days and weeks to follow. It still goes on for many people.

Because of that day of terror, 9/11 would always be a hard day for me. The memories flash, the news coverage shows those images again. It is hard for millions of people every year. Doesn't matter if it was three years ago or fifteen; it is one of those events in history that changed everything and if you were old enough to understand the seriousness and fright of that day and were able to comprehend that on that day, our country was under attack, 9/11 will always make your heart rush and put that lump back in your throat.

With those thoughts and feelings already in the forefront, I made my way down Interstate 80 in Nebraska, heading west toward the mountains five hundred-plus miles away. It seemed appropriate in hindsight that it all started on that day, with the storm of emotion building in me like a Midwest tornado, like an attack. To say that this was the scariest, worst drive in my life would be safe to say.

I was going to be alone now for days and had nothing but the thoughts in my head to be with. They have not exactly been a close friend lately, so the idea of being alone with "them" put me on edge for sure. I listened to my CDs and sung along best I could to try to take the sharpness out of me. I was going to my favorite place after all—my mountains! I repeated that to myself and tried to let it sink in, to take over the anxiety, stress, and doubt.

It did not really work.

Mile by mile, minute by minute, hour by hour, the self-doubt and anxiety got deeper inside of me. How could I think I could actually do this? What was I thinking? There was *no way* I could do this alone! I was scared out of my wits to even think about what I had to do.

Who did I think I was?

No! No! No!

I was having a full-on panic attack!

I could not breathe, so I rolled down the window. My heart was racing. I was sweating and shivering. I was saying something but had no idea what it was. It sounded like babble!

My eyes searched for the next exit, but in the middle of Nebraska, it could be miles …and miles.

Should I pull over? What should I do?

I drove on with every intention of finding the next exit and pulling over, turning my car around and heading home! Defeated and tail tucked between my legs but safe and protected. I knew my husband would not judge me; he knew how incredibly hard this was for me.

I could figure out something else.

Another time, with someone along maybe, I would figure it out. I just could not do this, not right now. I was not ready.

As I looked anxiously for a green or even a blue sign telling me when the next exit was, a car came up past me in the fast lane. It was going at least fifteen miles over the speed limit and cruised past me. Then it pulled over into the right lane in front of me and slowed down. The car slowed down so much I had to tap my cruise control and gas the car myself. Before I knew it, I actually tapped my breaks so I would not hit this obnoxious driver! Nothing makes me more frustrated than a tapped break on the interstate! It is so unsafe!

I could not to this day tell you what kind of car it was or even what color it was painted.

But I can tell you this: as I pulled up behind it, trying to keep my safe distance, I was able to read the license plate.

The license plate said, "L BELL."

I stared at it for a minute, trying to wrap my head around what I was seeing.

Was this panic attack causing hallucinations? Did this car that just almost cut me off on the interstate really have a vanity plate that said the nickname that my dad gave me? Did it really read Elle Belle?

I started to laugh! Are you kidding me? Real subtle, Dad!

I laughed and cried at the same time. I am sure if you were in that car with me, you might have said I was losing it, that it was hysterical laughter. I had finally lost it! But that was not the case.

I was laughing because it comforted me right when I needed it most. The laughter erased all the anxiety and my panic attack away. If this is not a clear message from beyond, from my dad, then please tell me what else it was. Coincidence? Remember my theory on that … No, this was a sign when I needed it.

It was a confirmation that "Yes, Laurie, you are able to do this, and you have to do this. I am here with you now, and I will be with you the entire way. We will get through this together."

I pulled myself together and cleaned up my tears both from laughing and from the fact that I felt my dad there with me. He had never let me down while he was on this planet, and he would never let me down even in heaven. His voice rang in my head. "You are stronger than I am, Elle." His blue eyes stung my memory.

I put both hands on the wheel at ten and two, straightened my crown, and drove on.

I was going to do this, and it was going to be okay. If I did it with love in my heart and for the two men that I missed in my life, whom I felt were taken from me before I was ready to say goodbye,

I could do it. I was lucky, and I knew it. I did get the chance to say goodbye to both of them. I just was not ready to yet, but I was working on it …

This trip was one more way to say goodbye to them and for them to know exactly how much I was willing to do for that love. I would climb mountains and walk for miles. I always would if I was able to.

I drove for miles and hours and finally started to get closer to the mountains. I finally got to the point where you can see the mountains in the distance. I waited for the relief to wash over me, but it didn't. I guess I needed to be closer, to be able to see the peaks in the distance.

As I wound into the valley and started to smell the pine and feel the sun, I waited for the tears. I *always* got tears in my eyes when I got to and when I left the Rockies! *Always*.

Not this time. Not yet at least. Interesting.

Was it because of the mood of the trip? Because it was so serious? Nevertheless, I was ready to get to my destination, to get to my room, to get to my Rocky Mountain Park.

It was late afternoon when I got in to Estes Park. I stopped at the grocery store and got milk and the cold items that I did not pack and went to check into my cabin. As I drove up to the registration office, a truckload of memories tried to run me down.

I went to the office and collected my keys, the clerk trying to make small talk with me. I was not very vocal. I was trying to keep it all together.

I went to the cabin and put my items inside. The cabin was perfect. It was right next to a babbling brook with a porch facing it. It had two beds and a mini kitchen with a wood-burning fireplace and a fresh stack of wood outside. It felt rustic and mountains, just like I needed.

No flood of relief yet. Jeez! Was it going to be like this the whole trip? Or just until I spread the ashes?

I was feeling anxious again and felt smothered. I decided to head into the park and drive to the falls that my husband and I were married next to. We were underneath a couple huge pine trees, and there was nowhere more romantic. That should bring me comfort. I just needed to see my peaks and valleys again—my heart's home. That would bring me that familiar "Aahhhh" moment I got when in my mountains.

After unpacking the car, that was exactly what I did.

I drove in to Rocky Mountain National Park and, from the entrance, drove up to Many Parks Curve. It is this area that, in the winter, is usually as far as you can go up the mountain due to the snow. It was open all the way to the top at this time of year but seemed like a good place to stop for the day. I looked out into the valley from the mountaintop and was awed by the size and beauty. As many times as I have been there, it still never disappointed.

I drove back down the mountain and decided to wait in the aspen grove by the falls until dusk. At dusk, I would be able to see the elk move down from the high country and maybe even see some bighorn sheep come down to the salt lakes. That was the plan at least. I parked in the rest area next to some picnic tables and got out. I walked away into the aspen grove and breathed in the wood and mountain air. I breathed deep and hard over and over again.

Then I laid down on a fallen pine tree and stared into the sky. As I looked up into that blue mountain sky with the quaking aspen leaves breaking up the deep hue and creating a striking contrast with its own gold pigment highlighted by the sun as they shook, I found a crack, a very small but definite crack into my state of anxiety and tension. The deep breathing and the familiar landscape that led to my peace so many times in the past had allowed me to feel it.

Briefly.

It seems I had lost it as fast as I found it. I spent a lot of time after that initial feeling trying to find it again, but instead I found despair. Instead I found overwhelming sadness and unbelievable apprehension about what the future held.

I wept very hard on that tree that day. Body shaking, weeping— which I had not done since my father died—it all came flooding out of me, and I melted into a heap of sobs and tears. I was exhausted and drained from the day.

I spent some more time there, forcing myself to try to enjoy the space, to enjoy the fresh air and sunshine. I was forcing myself to look around, be in that moment there in the mountains. There was nothing organic about it, though. There was nothing natural about it.

I was putting on an act that I did not enjoy, an act in a movie that was still developing, and nobody really knew what was going to happen and how it would end. Was it a drama? Was it a love story? Was it an action movie? What if it ended up being a comedy? Or worst yet, what if it ends up being a documentary or a disaster film?

It was all unsure, and isn't that what really causes us to worry—the unknown? I had a rough plan, but the rest was all improv. That is some scary stuff. Ask any comedian or actor.

My plan about watching the elk and sheep was shelved until the next night. I was too tired to do much more in the mountains that day and really needed some downtime in my room before building a fire and trying to sleep. I drove back to the lodge and back to my room. I took a small walk down to the creek and around the resort and familiarized myself with the area. It was a really beautiful place, and I loved walking around and enjoying the scenery.

I had a bite to eat and settled on the porch to finish a book I had been reading for a few months.

I sat listening to the creek and the wind howl through the mountains and tried to read. I was reading on a Kindle with that particular book and wanted to finish it so I could move on to another book I was excited to start, a Stephen King book.

I had a very hard time concentrating enough to read though. I kept having to reread the sentence or paragraph because my mind would wander to the task I had in the days to come. I felt like a puppy trying to not notice all the squirrels running around in a park. I would find myself staring at the water or sky when I was just reading last time I remembered. Then I would ask myself what I just read. Those last couple chapters of that book took me forever to read.

Part of the reason it took so long is because the doubt and anxiousness had started to creep in again. I wondered what I was doing. Here I am, five hundred miles away and all alone. What was I thinking? I started to believe that this whole trip had been a big mistake. My lack of belief in what I was doing was causing me to lose faith in why I was there too. I felt selfish and dishonest about what I was doing. It was all a secret after all. What was the reason for that? That was never a good way to start anything, in secrecy.

I looked inside myself and decided that what I was doing was weak and self-serving. I started to question whether this had been my brother's wishes or mine.

This conflict with myself was a real struggle and demanded to be addressed.

I was losing strength to fight all these internal doubts and questioning. The heaviness started to settle in again.

I somehow made it to the last few pages of the book. It was a good book, and I did enjoy it. But it was starting to feel like I did not do it justice in the end. I zombied my way through the last few chapters and did not get the full effect that the author had in mind when bringing it to the exciting ending he had planned.

I was having too difficult of a time concentrating and did not allow myself to be swept away to another part of my mind, where creativity and imagination ruled. I decided I would reread it someday in a few years when I have forgotten the end.

If you have ever read a Kindle or electronic book you know that to advance a page on the book, you push a tab on the side to go back and forth pages. It gives a percentage on the bottom so that you also know how far you have gone in the book. It's the only way you can really tell how much more is left since you can't just flip ahead and glance through chapters. Electronic books take some getting used to, but they have their place. They can be very convenient.

I must admit, though, that I still like the senses you use with an actual book more—the touch, the smell, the weight that helps to set up a sense of accomplishment that you finished this big old book you have been lugging around with you everywhere. I am an old-fashioned reader; that is for sure. But I believe in any type of reading. Exercise for the brain is what it is.

As I said, I was struggling through the last few chapters of a book I had been reading for several months now. I was sitting on my mountain porch and waiting for the sun to go down, still finishing my book. I had gotten to the part of the book where the author says a few things about the book, its inspiration, creative start, stuff like that. I had gotten done finally.

I read that last part, "Afterword." And I tabbed forward to the end. It ended with the author sincerely thanking his reader, and when I tabbed to the last page, it ended with the date he had written the end sentence.

The date he finished the book and afterword—the date was on the last page.

It was the only thing on the last page. It had broken up electronically so that only the date was left. It read: "September 14, 2009."

September 14, my brother Mark's birthday, the day I would be spreading his ashes. September 14.

Now remember, I had started reading this book months ago—before I had this trip planned, before I knew I would be up in the mountains alone, before I knew that I would need encouragement from the other side, before even I lost my dad.

The universe, in its amazing way of keeping the rhythms of life in balance and showing us we are on the right path, had somehow made it happen so that right when I needed it, my brother was able to send me a message. What bigger message than his birthday, his day to have his final wishes carried through!

Now I knew he would be there with me. My dad and him both would be there for me. I felt that now. This was my brother's license plate moment.

After picking my jaw off the ground, I smiled. I smiled on my face, and I smiled in my heart.

Mark was there for me when I was having fear and trepidation about what I was doing, just as my dad seemed to be there on the interstate when I was so close to turning around. I truly believe that these little nudges were to help me do what must be done. They were confirmations that I was on my chosen path in life at that moment.

The sheer planning by the spirits to have me read that book and finish it on that exact date at the exact moment when I needed it most cannot be explained by anything else in my opinion. The odds on that being a coincidence are incalculable.

For the rest of the night, I felt good. I built a fire, and I felt a positive wave come over me. The negative feeling was starting to have less of a hold on me. I could maybe even start to believe that. I could feel more of that weight being lifted off me.

My brother's birthday date on my Kindle was another one of those moments that if I didn't see it, I would not have believed it. But it had set the tone for my faith. I better start to believe it; that is what it said. It was another slap by the universe's hand, a slap that was helping to wake me up.

As I sat staring at the flames and smelling the fresh sap and bark and hearing the crackling of the wood, it felt right. I saw it all. I heard it all. I smelled it all. I was in that moment. I slept very good that night and barely remember any dreams or nightmares for that matter. For me, that was an accomplishment.

The next day was my day. I was planning on taking a somewhat easy hike to Fern Lake and soaking in my mountains for all I could. It was my soul-scrubbing day!

The only ghost I had to think about was the fact that it was my brother Dan's birthday. I was very close to where he lived, only one hundred miles or so. But I had already made the decision that I would keep to myself, even if it was a selfish decision. I needed these days alone to mentally, spiritually, and physically prepare for why I came up there. My brother would just have to understand. And somehow, I knew he would. He always understood what a mountain girl I was and knew there had been trips up there before when I was alone that I did not let him know about. He also knows I am a spiritual being and that I always had certain "beyond this world" beliefs.

And let's face it. He is an artist too, so he can totally relate. I mean, they are his mountains too. Love you, Dan!

September 12 started with me packing up my car for a hike and a day in the mountains. It started early by 7:00 a.m. I was at the start of the trail. I was able to park close to the trailhead instead of having to take a shuttle or walk a long distance just to get to the trail. It is a popular hike because you pass ponds and waterfalls along the way that are easy for kids to do or for not-so-experienced hikers to maneuver and it's very beautiful of course. The trail also follows the Big Thompson River and connects with other water sources, so it is also a popular spot for fly-fishing.

It was a glorious day of warm temperatures and very little cloud cover. Just a light wind, so hearing the bugling elk was very easy. I stood on the edge of a valley and recorded the view in a 360-degree video on my phone that I look at often. It is the epitome of peaceful.

It was just such a perfect mountain day!

Since I got an early start, I was able to watch the light come over on to the mountains in that creeping, alluring way that seemed to say, "What are you going to do with this amazing new day I am giving you?" The day seemed to slowly unfold with the sunshine that started to fill the ten thousand-foot-plus mountain range.

The first good stop was Cub Lake. It is a magical lake that is filled with lily pads and trees in every direction. It is truly a pond you would see in a fairy tale, a pond that would have sprites and the lights of fairies flying everywhere. It even had fog in some areas where the sun had not burned it off yet.

Next to this spiritual water are rocks the size of houses. It shows the power of nature in such a startling way when you notice the extreme difference in the rugged huge rocks that have torn their way off the side of a mountain millions of years ago, only to end up next to this mystical and fragile environment.

As I said, it is a very popular hike to go on for families and such. With that being said, even at that early hour, I stopped only briefly for a drink and watched the ducks for a moment before heading off down the trail. I wanted the opposite of people around me right now. I felt people at this point would steal away from me whatever it was I felt I was doing. Doesn't make sense to me either. But I stepped right past that lake and headed for the falls.

It is such a great hike with well-maintained trails until you get past the falls. Then it is kind of a "Am I still on the trail?" situation at times. But the walk to the falls goes past aspen groves and pine trees that are sixty to eighty feet high. The air is clean. You can hear a hawk or elk cry thousands of feet away. It follows water the whole time, so you hear the water babbling through the rocks next to you. There are many wildflowers and beautiful rocks. It is "Colorful Colorado" after all!

Impressive Fern Falls is a sixty-foot drop waterfall that comes down from the mountaintop where snow melted and overflowed and filled Fern Lake, thus creating the falls. It is a great accessible waterfall and is easy to stand right next to from the trails and rocks they set up.

I scrambled up the falls to a higher-up spot I could explore and enjoy my breakfast at. It is a fun climb because it is a very heavy rock-to-rock-over-water experience. And it smells amazing with the water splashing on the greenery and leaves falling into the water. It humbles me with its power and breathtaking beauty.

I found a place to set up a snack on a rock by the water. It was very private, and nobody could see me from the trail although I could see and hear them. It was very mountain lion–like.

I heard some interesting things. I will tell you that. But mostly I was alone with nothing but the wind, water, rocks, and elements speaking to me. It was exactly what my soul needed, and I felt the rush I get from the mountains. I actually felt as if I was starting to really feel stronger and being nourished in my mind and heart.

Although I have said several times that this is an easy hike and that is why it is so popular, that is not exactly true. It is easy to a certain point. But all in all, it starts at an elevation of 8,155 feet above sea level, and in a series of switchbacks and rock climbs, you will gain 995 feet to Fern Lake that is at 9,050 feet above sea level. It is a 3.8-mile hike both ways. It can be a challenge for sure.

After I sat and had my snack, I started back up the trail.

I passed two little kids around the ages of five or six. I asked them, "Where are your parents?" And they walked right past me, showing me the respect all youth seem to have for adults these days.

I got sterner and said, "Hey! I asked you where your parents were?"

And they stopped and turned around and said, "Behind us somewhere."

I started toward them and told them to stay where they were. I went over and told them that the mountains were no place to be walking alone when you were so little.

"First of all, you were both quiet," I said. "You should always try to make noise, talk, or get a stick like mine and hit things from time to time." I explained that the last thing you want to do is surprise a bear or look like prey to a mountain lion.

There was actually a sign on this trailhead that stated that there had been lion sightings and to be extra cautious.

As I was speaking to them, asking their names and small-talking with them, their parents came up.

It was two women who were out with the kids and having some girl time, you could tell. They were deep in conversation and barely noticed me standing there with the kids. I stopped them, and I have to admit, I lectured them like they were my own children.

"Are these your kids?" I asked.

They said they were, and I asked, "Do you want them to disappear, get lost, or get eaten by a bear, or are you just not fully aware of the dangers in these mountains?"

Blank stares. That was what I got—blank, who-just-slapped-me-in-the-face stares.

I told them that I had noticed the kids walking alone and gave them a list of reasons why this is such a dangerous thing to allow them to do.

I vocalized, not so kindly, to them, "If you want to go on a walk with your girlfriends, then do it. Don't drag your kids around the mountain as bait."

Okay, that was kind of mean. I admit it.

But nothing makes me madder than people not respecting the power of the animals and elements in the mountains. This is not a park in the city you are power-walking in. This is a wild environment. These are the Rocky Mountains.

So I left, saying, "Next time, be more careful."

I did not give them a chance to say anything. That was a good thing, I am sure, because I was in a pounce mood for sure.

They probably thought I was crazy, but it is a sore spot with me when I see children who are not being taught to explore but respect Mother Nature like I was taught, not to mention at my age at this point, life itself is very precious to me. Everyone's lives. So protect it when you can.

Was I out of line? Maybe.

Was I rude? A little.

Was I harsh? Oh yes, I was. I gave them tongue lashings, no doubt.

I wanted them to think about what I was saying. At times, I really do think these mountains are mine and I have to protect them, protect them from selfish people.

Oh yeah, and protect those children too. To be honest, that's not really my responsibility; that falls on their parents. But I will always defend my mountains and give them the respect and awe they deserve.

I continued on the hike up and up, back across the trails switches, across large boulders and rock paths thick with pine needles under my feet. The day started to warm as the shadows got longer. It sometimes takes the sun a little while to get past the peaks.

As I went, I took a couple layers off, stopping wherever there was a clearing to see spectacular views of the valley. I stayed close to the water whenever the trail gave me that option. It was a really great hike, and I finally made it to Fern Lake—my final destination for the day. The trail system in Rocky Mountain National Park is so amazing. From Fern Lake, there are three or four different hikes you could continue on and do in different directions, each with its own awe-inspiring finish.

I found a large flat boulder the size of a car to sit on, basically in the lake, because I had to walk over several large boulders in the water to get to mine. There I sat with prefect postcard views in all directions. You could count the number of clouds you could see on one hand. It was a gorgeous day in the mountains!

That hike felt weird because although I saw people and said "Hello" and "Nice day" and all that stuff and even stopped to talk to some of them (and scold a couple), I felt very alone that day, which was good, which was what I craved and wanted and needed. I felt small and simple in the magnificence of the mountains.

I will never be able to describe in any kind of descriptive, touching. or awe-inspiring way how beautiful it is there. But here goes.

Imagine a crystal clear dark-blue lake with the brightest lights shimmering off the top in the shapes of the waves drifting slowly across the water from the breeze. They are so bright because you are closer to the sun there. You can feel that on your face as well. Directly out of this ethereal lake are mountain peaks, most of which reach above the tree line. Surrounding these peaks are other mountain peaks. There are glaciers over ten thousand years old in some of these peaks and rocks.

Rocks and rocks and rocks. It is the Rocky Mountains—that is obvious.

But you see, there's life amongst the rocks up there too. Every once in a while, you will see a stray tree or greenery growing out of a rock. It is small and has struggled for a long time just to get to its tiny existence. But it shows you that even in the harshest environment, precious life continues to go on. It tries at least.

There are perfect conditions for life in this unforgiving landscape, like below the tree line. And then there are imperfect conditions, like above the tree line.

But it still tries. Life still forces itself into the world if it can find a way even when it is such an impossibility just to stay alive at this altitude. Life does not care; it wants to live. It reminded me how important that fact is when I sat there, right on the edge of the tree line, right on the edge of life and no life in these mountains and at this altitude at least to see such things and just how very precious life itself is.

All lives.

It brings a strong feeling of being meek. We are all part of a bigger story intertwined together to keep one another at our best. Not just humans but all living things on this planet have a purpose, even spiders. Eeeck! *Shiver!* I hate spiders, but I know they have a purpose more than just creeping me out and giving me the willies …

I sat eating my lunch of granola bars, juice box, and jerky with cheese crackers, taking big deep mountain air breaths. It was a good hike, like I said, and it was helping to acclimatize my body for sure. I had broken out in a sweat many times on the way up and expected a workout on the way down too. Going down seems like it would be easier, and it does take less time because you do not have to stop so many times to catch your breath, but it is much harder on the knees and shins and legs in general.

It really is a breathtaking place—lots of deep green fern trees against all the color of the rock and blue sky. As I sat there, resting my body and getting some mountain sun, I looked around. I saw the Gable Mountain at 11,018 feet above sea level. It felt right up close and inviting me to come run up and climb—that is, until your mind starts to understand that those huge rocks were really thousands of feet away. The side of the mountain is loose gravel the whole way up, and it would actually take hours to get there.

As I sat there, I felt like I had been picked up and placed in the middle of a calendar or postcard because every which way you turned, it was even more stunning than the last.

I could also see Little Matterhorn at 11,586 feet, with a peak fitting the name. Turn from there, and you would see Knob top at 12,331 feet, just massive and impressive in every way. And also, one of my personal favorites, is Notch top at 12,129 feet. These mountains show how violent the earth must have been in pushing the ground around to form those mountains. It is really something to see.

They all had different looks and glaciers and snow and were spectacular. It was like climbing to the base of heaven and having lunch at the camp. It took my breath away and made my heart sing! My eyes and soul drank it in. I took a picture on my phone, but the image could only catch a glimpse of the actual beauty of being there.

I spent some time there, just thinking and not thinking, letting my brain go where it wanted to go. I was in the moment and enjoyed it very much.

I felt the attitude change in me start, and the mountain girl that I was deep down inside and always have been finally began to wake. The smells, the sights, the feels, the sounds—every sense was alive and running full blast ahead. This was a day I needed very much and for a very long time. I should have known better than to deny that from myself.

After a while, more and more people woke up and started showing up. That was my cue to start to head down. I had my alone time with my peaks, and for that, I was happy.

Heading down generally takes about half the time as going up obviously because you do not have to stop so often to catch your breath, mostly because of the altitude. But I made myself stop more often even on the way down. Usually, you are getting pretty tired at this point and just want to get off your feet and be done. But I was feeling like I didn't want it to end. I was going to take my time, so I stopped often.

There are many points and rocks you can climb on to catch the picture opportunity or catch your breath and look out on a sensational view, and I stopped at every one that did not have people there already. I would breathe the air, soak in the view, and feel the sunshine on my face. It was such a beautiful day, and I wanted to feel it to the fullest.

About halfway down, I decided to take a break. I had spied a spot on the way up that I found again and decided to climb over to it. It was off the trail and next to the stream where some huge boulders had fallen, creating a perfect little ledge out of sight and right next to the creek. It was even flat like a little table.

I climbed over to it and took off my gear and pulled out some snacks and water.

I remember it being super quiet except for the water. I could just close my eyes and listen to the water and the breeze down the peaks and almost hear voices—high-pitched voices like angels singing. I know that sounds weird, but that is the only way I can describe it. It felt like the water was forming words and telling me secrets. I have no idea what any of the words were, but they was calming and kind of rhythmic in the way it came together.

I started throwing leaves and sticks into the water and watching them float downstream, crashing into rocks or getting stuck along the way in a whirlpool. I watched them on their way to those little journeys and wondered where they would end up. Could they make it all the way to a lake or pass it by and be stuck in a tossing, tumbling existence down the side of the mountain?

I took a stick and put it in the water and stopped the flow of the creek. But not for long. The creek water always found its way past the sticks no matter how big the obstacle. It continued on its way down and over those obstacles.

That image struck me. That should be my goal. No matter what the obstacle, it can be passed. I put the stick in the water and sloshed it around, and the water turned muddy and dirty and continued down the mountain. But even as I watched, the water was pushing the dirty, messed-up water down and replacing it with pure mountain stream water. The stuff they make beer and bottle water from.

There it was, just keep pushing your way through the situation; it will clear up again.

Water is current and real just like life is, and it can get so messed up at times. But it will clear itself and push through.

It made me think that my life will not always have that muddy, can't-see-the-bottom-through-the-muck feel. Someday it will be smooth and clean, and I will see clear again right down to the rocks and pebbles on the bottom, in the water known as life.

The secret I am starting to learn is, you have to hold on. That's the key—holding on.

I sat there, playing in the water, learning life lessons in the mountains that day.

The way it hit me, those thoughts that I just had were so clear and comforting for some reason that I started to laugh in a "Well, there you go. How obvious is that?" kind of way.

I was full of relief and silliness and pride that the mountain was trying to teach me a lesson. I was proud that I had stopped, let it talk to me in its own way, and listened and understood what was being told to me. It is one of those memories now that helps me through difficult times, knowing it never lasts. The bad, and unfortunately, the good. It is a constant change—that is, as long as this big blue marble keeps spinning.

I came down the mountain and finally back to my car. I put all my gear away and took a cold drink out of the cooler. It was lunchtime, and I was going to go find a place to sit and eat the sandwich I made.

There is a picnic table area that only has a couple tables off the side of a valley; it is private and has the most amazing view. It is rarely free because it is the prefect picnic place. It is a hike from the highway, but just enough so that you are out of the car noise and can really feel and hear the mountains. I drove back the road toward Estes to check it out.

I lucked out that day because it was free! I sat and ate my lunch and watched the valley. I could see a small herd of elk from my spot. It was a younger male and had only a small harem of females. There were much bigger males in the park, so he would be lucky if he ended up with the ladies he had by the end of the season. He would hear an elk bugle off in the distance from time to time, but he rarely answered. I do not think he wanted to challenge any male or draw attention to himself. Love can be difficult in every species.

After lunch I drove back toward my room, stopping at a couple of hideaway spots that I knew of.

Oh yes, I was tired.

It had been a long day already with such an early start. I saw several herds of elk much bigger than the one I watched at lunch. I heard bugling and saw a couple struggles of power and stealing of females between the herds. It is always a sobering thought of how these creatures will have to endure the Rocky Mountains' winter and snow and freezing temperatures. The reality is some may not make it. All the living creatures in these mountains will be tested in the winter months and will hopefully see next spring.

Every life is a battle. Every life is a blessing.

I got back to my room that evening and called my brother Dan. Remember, all this has happened on his birthday.

I was successful leaving the guilt and burden of my trip behind while out in the mountains, but now back in the room, it started to creep in. I felt the burden of why I was there and the duplicity of nobody knowing, multiplied with the fact it was Dan's birthday. I reminded myself it was mucky now but that all clears up in the end.

I called Dan, and we talked about what he had done for the day. It was my usual birthday phone call to him. There was a Nebraska Cornhusker game that night, so after we talked on the phone, we continued our communication via text during the game.

I made myself a nice fire in the fireplace after walking down to the creek. It was a chilly evening, so a fire felt great.

I watched the Nebraska Cornhusker football game in my cabin and ate dinner. It had been a very physically draining day, and I was exhausted. It felt really good to be tired from my workout and hear the crackling of the fire. There was such a relaxing smell in the cabin, and I felt cleansed from my Rocky Mountains. I slept very well that night and did not see the end of that football game.

I woke up on September 13 refreshed from my hike the day before.

The plan today was to drive to the top of the mountains on Trail Ridge Road and continue to adapt to the altitude, so I would be ready, at least physically, for my hike to Lake Haiyaha the next day. How I would do emotionally and mentally was yet to be determined.

For those of you that have never driven Trail Ridge Road, also known as US Highway 34, it is forty-eight miles long, with eleven of those miles in the tundra vastness only found in a few places in the world. It gets you from Estes Park to Grand Lake through the most spectacular scenery you will see on this planet. Stop whatever you are doing right now and *go*!

Okay, maybe not. Keep reading this story because it starts to get really good from here on. Sorry. Spoiler alert. But make plans to go soon.

The US highway that was constructed in 1932 has breathtaking views and awe-inspiring vistas of some of the most beautiful scenery you can imagine. When originally constructed, Trail Ridge Road was only one way going up. Soon after they finished that road, they constructed the two-way version that is mostly used today.

When the first road was created, it was called the scenic wonder road of the world and has lived up to that name. The road has a grade of 5 percent but never exceeding 7 percent. It is a hairy beast of a road, and the pictures of the people brave enough to go up in in the early 1930s show some true adventurers of all kinds. This road is still open, still one way up, and still as hairy to drive as ever. It is called Old Fall River Road and should only be tackled by vehicles that can handle the roughness.

On Trail Ridge Road, there are many fourteen thousand-foot peaks to gaze upon, and you also see the ridgeline that is the continental divide on the west side. At its highest point of the road, you will be driving at 12,183 feet above sea level. You will experience an elevation gain of over four thousand feet and your ears will pop from the extreme altitude change. The roads are hairpin turns with very little obstruction on the side of the roads to interfere with the amazing views.

That also means it is some stressful yet thrilling driving. You are right on the edge of the road at times with little between you and literally falling off the side of a huge mountain cliff. It is not for the faint of heart, unless they close their eyes.

It is one of my most favorite places on earth.

On this road, you will experience different environments at different altitudes, experience different worlds, some you can only find in the most extreme places.

You will drive from aspen groves and ponderosa pines to large forests of fir and see waterfalls from the high country flowing down and crossing the road here and there. Then drive into a subalpine forest of spruces trees hundreds of feet high and thousands of years old until you reach above the tree line. Then on to the tundra, where you are basically in Arctic terrain. Be prepared for any and all kinds of different weather when driving in this park.

The tree line generally ends at ten thousand feet above sea level. Although like I said before, it's not like it's a straight line that just has trees below it and no trees above it, from a distance, although it can look like a pretty distinct line.

As I said, there is always that strong life force that tries to live on the edge, a little tree that somehow has found a tiny piece of dirt and ground that it can anchor its roots to and actually survives usually nestled in a rock. It actually beats all the odds and grows and reaches for whatever sun it can find and gets water from the snow and rain whenever it can. It also has to learn to tolerate extreme winds, some over sixty to eighty miles per hour. It has to make it through the Arctic cold because you are just around the corner from the Alpine tundra. And snow. Lots and lots of snow.

During the winter months, the snow in the high country is not measured in inches; it is measured in feet. There is a famous picture at the Alpine Visitor Center at the top of the mountain range that shows the very building you are standing in up there, the museum, in the winter. The snow goes over the roof with just an opening shoveled out for the crew to get in and out. Someone has to stay up there during all those unforgiving yet, I am sure, peacefully gorgeous months.

That was my final destination on this drive—the visitor center on top. I would not go on to Grand Lake but turn around and head back to Estes Park. Grand Lake is exactly that …grand. It is very deep and dark and a stark contrast to the green, almost blue, spruce that fill the mountainside around it. It is a good place to see moose, but my trip was not taking me that far.

If you have never seen the Colorado Rocky Mountains outside of Estes Park, then I (Rocky Mountain) highly recommend you put that on your bucket list. It will not disappoint and will give you an all-new view of life on this planet. If you ever want to feel little, go surround yourself by fourteen thousand-foot peaks. If you ever want your problems to seem like not such big problems, go and get close to the sky, above the clouds. It shows you who is really in charge.

I loaded up snacks and drinks and would get my traditional hot dog at the top. I know, gross, but there are only three places I eat hot dogs: at the zoo, at baseball games, and at the top of Rocky Mountain National Park Visitor Center. Maybe the occasional Omaha Steaks Hot Dog grilled out in the summer, but that was it.

I grabbed all layers of clothes because it got cold in the tundra. I grabbed gloves and boots; must be ready for snow up there. Once I was loaded up, I hit the road for my adventure. What would become of this mountain day? I felt ready. Was I?

Off I drove. Such a clear day thankfully, so should be good weather—at least at the starting altitude.

I took my time and enjoyed the views. I was in no hurry this day. Of course, the weather could change at any time, but I was ready for that too. That is what being in the mountains is all about, getting snowed on in June and sunburned in January. Mother Nature can be fickle at times, but never doubt she is in control the entire time.

The first place to stop and enjoy the lower hills is called Sheep Lakes or Horseshoe Park. It is called horseshoe because the creek that runs through it does half circles the whole way and looks like connecting horseshoes from above. The lake is where if you are lucky enough you will see bighorn sheep in the evening or morning come down and lick the rocks and area around the lake for the natural salt that develops.

I even saw a coyote den located there in the distance along the tree line one year.

It was so amazing to see the mother coyote come back and forth from the den with food. The little pups are all running in and out of the den, trying so hard to be brave and be the one who went the farthest away from the den before getting scared and running back to the safety of their home. They were so cute and little, looking so vulnerable out there alone in the wilderness when their mother was off hunting. I stood there with binoculars and watched them for over an hour. It's one of the many memories and gifts this mountain park has given me.

On this morning, there was nothing to see but a view of the sun coming and lighting up the peaks more and more as it rose.

Not too shabby, I would say.

The air was crisp, but I knew it would be a good day to be in the high country. I double-checked to make sure I had my sunscreen. Being closer to the sun is real up there, and a sunburn can happen pretty quick.

On my way back to the car, I saw a hawk circling above me. He was not too high up, and I remember I could see his coloring, the red of his tail, even the yellow in his beak. I am sure he was on the lookout for breakfast, but a good sign, I thought.

I drove down to Alluvial Fan, the impressive waterfall created by Lawn Lake flood in the '80s. This was the place where Greg and I were married and always a stop. We were married close to the falls but actually under two huge pine trees with an opening between them that we instantly both said looked like an altar and the perfect place.

It was chilly in the air still, so I only climbed a little bit on the rocks and watched the water rush down. It was a short walk next to the rushing water. The rocks were still cold, and I really did get shivery, not to mention the water coming down was just above freezing as well.

I continued down the road until I had to turn around. At the end of this road is Endovalley, which is a great picnic area. But if you wanted to continue up this road, you would be on the one-way Old Fall River Road. My little Chevy Cobalt is not the kind of car to take up this extremely scenic but dangerous road, especially alone.

But the picnic area is full of aspen and smells and looks amazing.

I parked and grabbed a juice box and breakfast bar and decided I would have breakfast here. I could think of no better place. It was sunny but chilly, and I could hear the breeze blow down the mountains. There were a few elks already bugling and sizing up the competition in chances that today they could increase their harem for the winter. It was so relaxing and releasing.

After I ate my breakfast bar and slurped the last of my juice box, I lay down on the picnic table. I lay there and watched the clouds and the blue sky dance together. I watched the aspen leaves quake and fall down, some right on top of me. It was September, and their golden time had almost come and gone for the year.

As I lay there, breathing in the mountain air, I also saw the hawk again. He was circling right above me and again so low I could see his coloring. He was a gorgeous hawk and was hungry, I was thinking. I wished him luck, went back to my car, and drove on up the mountain. I passed Beaver Ponds and went to Hidden Valley.

Hidden Valley is just what it sounds like.

It is a little valley that is off the road a bit and hidden between two big hills. One of the hills is covered with aspen and is a favorite spot for me to check out when I go to the mountains in the fall. Plus, not a lot of people know about it, so it is a good place to be alone.

I sat in my car, radio off. I never have my radio on while I am in the mountains; the sounds of the peaks are the only things I want to hear. I listened to elk and stared at the mountains, thinking about everything and nothing at all. I had my sunroof open and windows down. The breeze of the mountains was hitting me full blast.

It was then that I heard a screech. It was the screech of a hawk.

I looked up through my sunroof and saw not only one but two hawks now circling over me. It seemed my hawk had himself a buddy. Power in numbers is what they say, right? I smiled and wished them both good luck. Rabbits for them both! From Hidden Valley. I drove up past Many Parks Curve (I planned on stopping there on the way back) and up to Rainbow Curve.

I did that for two reasons. The parking is better at Many Parks Curve on the way down than up, and there were restrooms at Rainbow

Curve. The breakfast bar had kicked in. There were not many opportunities up there, so you had to take them when you could.

It was a greater altitude change up there too, and I was starting to get excited about being in the high country. Many Parks Curve is where the road closed from mid-October through Memorial Day due to snow. So in a month from when I was there, you would not be able to go as far as I could go that day.

Once I took care of business in the restroom, I walked back near my car. There is a rock wall that runs along the entire length of the parking lot. I sat on one of those stones of the wall and looked down on a truly spectacular view.

With my legs dangling over the side, I could see the entire valley. From here I could see the "horseshoes" of Horseshoe Park. I could see the Alluvial Fan waterfall. But from where I was, it appeared much smaller in size, but you could see all the way to the top of the waterfall.

You didn't get that view while down there next to it without a lot of climbing being done. At this point, you are more than two miles above sea level, more than 10,500 feet. After Rainbow Curve, you'd be starting to get above tree line.

As I sat there, looking at one of my favorite views, I listened to the people around me. I smiled as I heard many of them seeing it for the first time and saying how unbelievably beautiful it was. I enjoy hearing those conversations. Although I have seen this view more times than I can count, I feel joy hearing how it affects others seeing it for the first time.

I wish I could really remember how awestruck I was when I first saw this range of amazing vistas, but that was thirty-five years ago. I will tell you, I can still feel the impression they have left in my heart.

As I sat there, watching people take pictures and talking about the views they could see from there, a little chipmunk jumped on my lap.

He looked at me with his most cute eyes just in case I was eating something that he might like. The chipmunks up there are hardy for sure, and that sometimes comes from not being shy. They are not afraid of humans and usually scamper off once they realize you don't have food. I guess if you live at ten thousand feet and go through the winters they go through, there is not a lot that scares you.

But this little buddy seemed to be glad to see me even if I did not have food. He sat on my leg and started to clean himself and relax in the sun.

Mind you, he was doing all this on my jeaned leg.

The tourist around me all started to notice and ask if they could take a picture. It was a really weird thing. I kind of felt like Dr. Doolittle, very in tune with this little guy. I actually kind of was able to tune out everything around me and just hear the mountains.

I felt home. I felt peace—something that I have not felt for a very long time.

The chipmunk scurried away eventually, but in that moment, I felt very at one with nature. I felt very on the path I should be on.

And wouldn't you know it? As I looked up at the clouds before leaving, I saw two hawks just circling around, catching the breeze, certainly not at any altitude now to be hunting. They were way too high up for that. Was it the same hawks I have been seeing all morning? Who knew? It certainly felt like the same two. That was when it occurred to me. Were those two hawks Mark and Dad, keeping an eye on me?

It is a dangerous drive. It is an especially dangerous drive alone. I laughed it off as wishful thinking. I cried it off as hopeful thinking. Just another stage of my grief: trying to see signs that really are not there, I thought.

Then again, it felt like they have given me signs in the last few days, so why would this not be one too? Either way, it is always good luck and a beautiful thing to see soaring hawks in the mountains.

From there it was a climbing and winding road until you get to Forest Canyon. The drive is one of those things I find difficult to describe. You will be going past the most gorgeous scenery in all directions and will see something new every time you go up there.

Forest Canyon outlook is another premade rest stop to check out the views. This is a little hike off the road that leads to a perch overlooking many peaks and the continental divide. It is in the open, and I decided to let the day warm up a bit before going out there. It is a huge view, but you are exposed to the elements. I kept driving on.

I wanted to get to Rock Cut. I wanted to see Laurie Lake.

Rock Cut is appropriately named. The road literally goes through a rock that was blasted centuries ago to put in the road. It is cosmetically stunning, and I applaud them for doing it that way. It helps the road blend into the scenery. They did a great job with that, making this highway blend in and become a part of these mountains. Those early pioneers cherished these mountains as well.

There it was, my mountain range. I parked the car on the edge closest to the range and turned off the car. That was when I seemed to have turned on the waterworks. I cried. *Sobbed* is more like it.

I had gone so far to get here, mentally and physically, to where my heart soared. It was a cry of relief, fear, missing my loved ones, managing the flood of memories that were hitting me. All emotions all at once.

I stared at my peaks—Mount Julian at 12,928 feet next to Mount Terra Tomah at 12,718 feet, so colorful this time of year, with the golden grasses and deep green trees and every color of rock you could ever want to see. And my favorite Mount Ida at 12,880 feet looks and protects over my sparkling mountain lake.

Laurie Lake—at least that's what me and my family call it. It is really named Inkwell Lake and is the most beautiful mountain lake my eyes have seen. This is the lake I told Mark to spread my ashes at.

I know that will not happen now, but at least if somebody could stand on this rock wall and spread my ashes in the mountain breeze, I think I would find my way to Laurie Lake. I did a painting of this view, and it is still my most favorite painting. The detail I put in it and the hard work to blend the colors and make them just right were worth it. It is a beautiful painting to my eyes, if I do say so myself.

When I could get myself under control, I took the small hike up to the tundra trail. Although even a small hike at that altitude is a challenge, this is one of my favorites. Along the way, you see so many things you can only see there. The alpine ecosystem is rare and fragile. You can see mossy cushion plants in all colors growing as well as the tiny greenery. The growing season is short at that altitude, but they do thrive.

I love to stop and look at the tiny and colorful wildflowers that grow along the path. They're so delicate and pretty in detail, plus a good excuse to catch your breath at almost eleven thousand feet. There are a variety of birds and the ever-present yellow-bellied marmots too, and you do see elk this high up on nice days. When you get to the end of this trail, there are large rocks to climb up, and you get an outstanding view in all directions. You can see for literally miles and miles. It is worth the lack of oxygen and effort to get there.

I had been there with Mark many times, so I tried to touch where he might have touched and sat and thought about our time there. The sun was out and warm, so actually it was not as cold as it had felt earlier. It was cleansing to my heart and mind to be at this altitude. I am a mountain girl!

I walked back to my car, feeling refreshed, high, and strong. I was doing it. I was getting myself back. A part of me got shattered with grief and fear, and I felt so sure that this trip was exactly the right idea. I actually started to relax. I know I am driving in the mountains on treacherous roads, but I felt calm. I dare say I was anxiety-free for the first time since I could remember.

I went back to the car and grabbed something to drink and another snack to get me through until I had my hot dog. I climbed down over the rock wall and walked off a bit toward a huge rock pile. This is very fragile tundra terrain. I rarely will go on undesignated areas, and I do not encourage anyone to do so either. But I needed to be away from the people for a bit. Plus, I kept to the rock as much as possible to not create any damage.

I found a good place in the rock pile to nestle myself in, so I was partly out of the wind and could still see the glorious view. It was also a place that nobody from the road could see me as well.

I sat down, opened my water, and grabbed my snack. It was a hard-boiled egg. It had gotten very cold and was hard to peel, so some bits of it were still attached to the shell in areas. I left those tucked in the rocks for some lucky marmot or bird to find. Eggshells are biodegradable, and some form of bugs and insects will actually eat them. So I was not littering if that was your thought. It always amazes me how much life there is even at that harsh altitude.

After snacking, I sat for a long time soaking in the sight of my mountains and Laurie Lake. I thought back to the day with Mark that we were here and made our promise. I cried that I had the honor to do this for *him*. I cried because I *had* the honor to do this for him. I cried from fear, pride, relief, missing him and Dad, and just the beauty of where I was. It was a cleansing cry, and the mountain breeze blew my tears off my face at times. That felt like love and Mother Nature wiping my eyes. The rocks around me started to warm from my body, and as I leaned back, I felt like I was being hugged from the mountains themselves with the sun shining on me.

I finished my water. It's very important to stay hydrated in this environment, and I grabbed my trash and climbed out of my private space. I stood there for a minute, letting the cool, clean breeze blow in my face, and I looked up at the sky. I saw still a very blue sky that was filled with light cloud cover.

I saw something else too.

I saw two hawks flying up and down the valley that swept between the road and the huge peaks on the other side.

They would fly fast down the valley, spin, and slowly circle and meander their way back toward the north to the "top" of the valley and then fly fast with their wings tucked at their side down the valley. Then they would pull out of that fighter jet position and circle and float around on the wind current before doing it all again.

I had never seen hawks behave in such a military way. It was playful but almost felt like a competition they were having. I watched them do this maneuver a few times and laughed my head off. What was going on? I really was starting to wonder if these two hawks were my dad and Mark.

It was a strange yet entertaining and playful exhibition of their skills but something I would not consider normal hawk behavior.

Why do I keep seeing these hawks? It was getting to be more than a coincidence, and I really started to wonder.

Before I got back in my car, I took a selfie of me with my mountains in the background. When I later looked at that picture, I noticed that there were tears dried on my cheeks as little ice cube tears.

I must have been crying again when I was watching those hawks.

I got back to my car, and even though it was a very hard place for me to drive away from, I kept moving on. I had a hot dog waiting for me at the top, remember? Besides, I had taken a quite a few pictures at this stop, so I could always gaze upon them when I missed them terribly. I already missed them, and I was still here!

From Rock Cut, you go past Iceberg Pass next and on to the Lava Cliffs. I usually stop at Iceberg on the way down for parking reasons but love to stop at the Lava Cliffs. The road between these two stops is what I think of as the scariest. There are blind turns around mountainsides where you just hope that whoever is coming the other way is in their lane. There are no guardrails to keep you on the road; if not, it's just straight down and down and down.

They have sticks and poles in spots to measure the feet of snow, and so the snow plow can tell where the road is. Talk about a frightening job. No, thank you!

Lava Cliffs is such a cool stop—a little moonlike feel to it with winter snow and peaks in the background. You can see a huge frozen-in-time black dried lava cliff. It shows you once again the violence it took to create this amazing place. Great earth forces thrust the Rockies skyward 70 million years ago. But scientists think that these lava explosions happened just 1.3 million years ago.

This is a good place to recognize that we are on a living thing. This earth is doing its evolving, and we cannot stop it. We can change it and increase it, like in climate change for example, but ultimately this planet will do what it needs to survive and thrive. With or without us humans on it.

There are snow glaciers around this lava that are millions of years old. I remember once while I was out there, the Colorado Mountain

Rescue Team was out on them and doing their ice pick climb drills. It was an amazing sight to see. They looked so deceptively small; it really helped to put the enormousness of these mountains into perspective. From the road, they look large. But put a human on one for scale, and you see how huge they really are. It was so impressive to see them at work too—true heroes and such strong people, physically and mentally, because what they were doing was scaring the wits out of me and I was safely in my car, just watching.

After getting past the Lava Cliffs, you drive up even further and get to the highest point on the road. There is no fanfare, no stop-and-get-out-and-take-pictures area, just a little sign. I miss it sometimes while I am driving up; that is how subtle it is. At this point, you are 12,183 feet above sea level. That is the equivalent of 2.37 miles. If you are susceptible to any kind of effects from altitude, you will know it now. I am lucky in that I thrive in these conditions. I have been up there with others who do not, and it is hard on the system for sure.

From there, the next stop is Gore Range. This is the best view of the continental divide and the Never Summer Mountain Range. It is a very educational stop and gives you the names of all the mountain peaks you are gazing upon and the history. This park has seventy-two peaks above 12,000 feet and several above 14,000. It is a feast for the eyes, mind, and soul.

My next stop was my last stop. The Alpine Visitor Center at 11,796 feet. This was two buildings up at the top of the road before heading down again toward Grand Lake.

One building had a really neat museum that was extremely educational. They had some amazing historical images of those early mountain days as well as facts about the wildlife that called that area home.

The other building was a gift shop that also had a food-and-sitting area. Hot dog, here I come!

They were nestled atop a bowl in the mountain where you could see down into the valley and spot wildlife and the old Fall River Road. There was a glacier in this bowl that was thousands of years old. I have often seen elk and bighorn sheep in this bowl. It faces the east, with the north being blocked by the buildings and rock wall, so it was an excellent place for them to eat and rest and stay out of the elements.

There is also a restroom and a hiking trail called Alpine Ridge Trail that was a very long stairway up the peak so when you reached the top, you were above twelve thousand feet. It is very popular and always has people going both up and down. I decided to skip this one, but I did hit the restrooms before going to the gift shop.

I had decided that I was going to get a new long-sleeved T-shirt, something for Greg and the pets, of course, and my usual souvenir of a hemp wish anklet.

I was looking at the shirts and had found a new one that I liked when a lady asked me what I thought of the one she found. I laughed and told her I loved it, because I actually already had it. It was a shirt that had all the trails listed on the back and a mountain view and "Rocky Mountain National Park" on the front at the top as an emblem.

She had laughed back and said, "Well, I guess it's a winner."

She then went on to gush over how lovely and spectacular the park was, and I acknowledged that I agreed 100 percent.

"That is why I have been coming here for thirty years to scrub my soul when I need it," I said.

She looked at me with what I would describe as a shocked look and said, "Oh my gawd, that is exactly what it is. I am going to use that. Do you mind?"

She was obviously from the East coast because she talked like a New Yorker even at this altitude. I told her she could use that phrase whenever she wanted.

"You are very wise for such a young woman."

Now it was my time to laugh again. "I am not as young as you would think. The mountains make me feel young so …"

Mind you, I am in full mountain girl mode—no makeup, probably barely brushed my hair or it was in a ponytail. I was pleased with the thought of still feeling young and maybe even looking a little young at least.

I figured out what to bring Greg and the animals. Then I looked for my anklet. They usually have them on the checkout counters and are impulse items. I could not find one though.

This was terrible. This was my tradition, and I always got one to make a wish with every time I came to my mountains. Of all the trips, this was the one I really needed to have a wish made on. I kept looking around but still didn't find one. I did find a new bumper sticker to replace the one on my car that was faded out. It was the exact same one of Bear Lake, so I could just place it right over the faded one. But no wish bracelet.

I asked someone who worked there if he knew where the bracelets might be. He was a European young man who was just there working for the season. He had come a long way to be in the Rockies. He did not even really understand what I was asking for, but with a little help from another worker, we ended up finding them.

Whew! It would have felt very wrong to not get one. In fact, I still have it on my ankle as I write this. My wish has still not come true. Only the mountains and I know what that wish is.

As he was ringing me up, he started asking where I was from, if this was my first time up here, etc. After I told him of my history of being up there, he confessed it was his first time living and working in the Colorado Rocky Mountains summer season. He was intending on staying in the mountains and finding a ski resort to work in for the winter. He told me that he had been to a lot of places but had never seen anywhere so grand in his life.

Grand—that is a word you rarely hear someone use but is amazingly appropriate.

It was then that he asked me what my plans were for the rest of my trip, if I was hiking any trails, and if I could recommend any to him. I told him what trail I was going on the next day and why I was going.

I even told him it was Mark's birthday the next day. I am not sure why I even told him; it always felt so good to talk about my brother. I wanted everyone to hear his name and remember him—people who knew him and strangers alike.

That was when this young man said something to me I will never forget.

"You are a good sister," he said. He had tears in his eyes when he said it.

"Well, thanks, I may be a good sister, but he was the best brother," I answered.

The tears in his eyes rolled down his cheeks then. We smiled at each other. He told me to be safe, and I told him to enjoy his time here in Colorado. Then I left.

It was one of those strange moments. It was an encounter with a stranger that happens in your life that you will never forget. It is always an amazing thing when I think ever so briefly about people in my past whom I have met or interacted with, even for the smallest amount of time, and have had such a direct impact on me. You can sometimes not really see clearly that this person has impacted you until time has passed. That's what makes it not so random. I took my purchases and headed for the snack bar.

Gross, nasty hot dog, here I come! I was super excited, I have to admit. Actually, it really is pretty good. I put the cheese sauce from their nachos on it to make it extra bad for me. Hey, you know, at this altitude, you burn more calories, and your body needs to be stronger to survive. We don't judge above tree line.

I took it to go. I wanted a better view to eat it in. I drove back down to Gore Range after putting on my new bumper sticker and had lunch there.

It is a really cool view for me there because, at that angle, you see the backside of Mount Ida. Just looking at it, I know Laurie Lake is right over that peak. There were lots of people out on the pathway and ledge where the trail ended, and they all looked cold. The wind really comes crawling down right on top of you at that point out there. You are exposed in all directions.

The view is awesome from the car too though. I am just saying.

I sat there and ate my hot dog with nachos cheese sauce and a bag of chips and looked out at all the different views in front of me. Soul scrubbing—that was exactly was I was doing. I was this little speck of a person who was here to do something very special but had no real meaning to the world, just my family's world.

I felt strong (it might have been the hot dog), and I felt like, yes, not only was I a good sister, but I was a good person—a unique person who was a lot stronger than I ever give myself credit for. I mean, there I was above the tree line, all alone with only my thoughts. To be alone is a very scary thing to a lot of people, and I recognize that. And I am not talking about being alone without anyone who cared or loved you. Yes, of course, that is the worst existence imaginable. But to love and understand yourself enough to be your own company, to be your own traveling companion, to have the courage to be alone, I was glad that I had the opportunity to do this, and I really enjoyed it. I actually think that it was on this trip that I started to love myself again.

I was so wrapped up in what I had lost and how I would change. I was consumed by how much it was going to suck not having them around (hello, pity party for one) that I was not able to see to the core of who I really was, the things about me that they both loved. You have to love yourself to love anyone else, right?

Love had betrayed me twice by taking away a piece of my heart. A piece of me was torn out of me when I lost my brother, and another piece of me was sliced away when I lost my dad. I had decided not to love because it was too dangerous. Of course, I loved my family, husband, and friends still. But I did not love life. I did not love what the rest of my life was going to be like now.

That's life as they say. It took me being alone with my own thoughts and my own risks and freedoms and free will to start to see that. Scrubbing my soul is *exactly* what I was doing.

Scrubbing away some of the grief grime that had accumulated by my all-consuming losses. Maybe my soul would shine again if I kept following what felt like to me this first step. They loved me for a reason too. I needed to find that girl again.

At over 11,000 feet, looking at my mountains! I think my heart has finally begun singing again! My heart is getting healed, and I feel like I am getting stronger. I have had a few anxiety ridden moments and asked myself what the hell are you doing ... but right here, right now I understand. My soul was yearning for this and I am glad I listened to my own advice. I had a hard, awesome hike up Fern Lake yesterday. Going hiking again tomorrow to release part of Dad, Mark, and Alpine in the high country where they can soar like the young hawks I saw this morning! Therapy and release is what it is. Love and miss you two always. That I know will never change. Now, back to the Rockies!

After a while, I decided to keep moving on. Belly full of lunch, I was ready. I pulled over several times to take pictures or just soak in the view. I was in no hurry, and the longer I stayed at this altitude, the better. It had turned out to be a decent day, and although clouds were rolling down the mountains, it remained mild. So it was not too painfully cold even with the cloud cover. I pulled over at one stop before I left the Never Summer Range view and sat on the side of the road. As I sat there, breathing the fresh air, I saw them again.

Two hawks were soaring side by side over the canyon.

They were so high up that at times I could not see them. When they went sideways to turn, they were merely a slit in the air and very easy to lose until they soared horizontally again. They were a feast to my eyes though. I felt safe and protected. It seemed that whoever these two hawks were, they seemed to be keeping an eye on me. In my gut, of course, I thought they must be Dad and Mark. Wishful thinking maybe, but odd nonetheless.

I stopped at most of the places I had passed on the way up as long as there were not too many people and, of course, spent more time at Rock Cut to see my mountains and Laurie Lake one more time. I doubted I would be back up here again since I was going home the day after Mark's birthday. You never know, but just in case, I memorized every crack and color and image of this mountain range with my brain as I possibly could.

I shed some tears. I laughed at some memories, and I glanced back over my shoulder and in my rearview mirror several times as I finally drove away. My heart will always stay in those mountains, though my body must leave it.

I drove down the mountain, and my last big stop was Many Parks Curve.

I had been coming here for decades, remember? So this particular stop has really changed. It used to be just a pull-off to climb some rocks and check out the views, but now it has a parking lot and wooden plank pathway all along the east side. The pathway goes from the parking lot to the original rocks that first drew people to stop here. It is a beautiful view that shows all the valley, including Estes Park itself.

I parked my car down by the original rocks. It is a much smaller parking area, but that's where I prefer to park. I am old school, and that is where I parked when I was twenty. That was where I want to park now that I was fifty. I got out and climbed the rocks as usual. But then I climbed off the rocks and down into the trees, catlike again, and just got out of sight. I sat there and thought about my day and smelled the pine and fir and was thankful for such a majestic day. I was given many gifts from the mountains on this day, and I felt blessed.

I eventually climbed out of the trees and decided to walk along the wooden pathway and check out the view. I actually walked on the rock wall about three feet high that lined the road. I was in full mountain mode, and that sometimes brings the kid out in me. There were aspen trees that line the hill and came right up to the pathway. I stopped and stood between two big aspens and hugged them both. Yes, I am a tree hugger! I leaned close to them and breathed deep. I love the smell of aspen!

As I gazed down into the valley and looked around at all the different parks and peaks I could see from this vantage, I also looked up to the clouds.

There he was—a hawk soaring on the breeze.

I smiled and felt privileged that my hawks were still hanging around. Don't get me wrong. I have seen plenty of hawks in the mountains. It is not exactly a rare sighting. But I have never in all my times going up there seen hawks with this kind of frequency and consistency, maybe once or twice a trip, but never almost every time I looked up in the sky the whole day long.

As I watched that hawk flying in the sky, he flew past the sun. For just one brief second, I saw something.

I looked up in that direction again, and with my sunglasses on, I looked in the direction of the sun and blocked it out with my thumb so I would not burn my eyes.

There it was. I could see a rainbow around the sun. Actually, there were two rainbows—one on top and one upside down on the bottom.

I know it was a natural phenomenon, but what were the odds of me seeing it, of me noticing those rainbows right when I needed to see rainbows and sunshine in my life? Those are two things that you do not see together like that very often—full sun and rainbows.

As we all know, rainbows usually come after rain and are a result of reflection from that moisture left behind. In fact, definition of a rainbow is this: "A rainbow is a meteorological phenomenon that is caused by reflection, refraction and dispersion of light in water droplets resulting in a spectrum of light appearing in the sky. It takes the form of a multicolored arc. Rainbows caused by sunlight always appear in the section of the sky directly opposite the sun."

It had not rained all day, not one drop. So much for the reflection-of-water idea.

I have looked up what a rainbow around the sun means. They are called halos.

As in angel halos? Well, maybe, if you consider religious art. The Bible does not mention anything about halos on angels, but artists for centuries have drawn and painted them with halos. Interesting to me at this moment is that I see one.

Also, it's interesting because sun halos are caused by high cirrus clouds that form ice crystals on them and when they pass by the sun, they leave ice particles in the air that cause these halos. There had been no clouds in the sky since hours ago.

It was such a crazy thing to notice that I shared it with others walking along the pathway if they had on sunglasses.

"Do you want to see something cool?" I would ask them. Then I'd instruct them to block out the sun and tell me if they could see the rainbows.

"Wow!" was what the first set of ladies I stopped said to me. "Thank you for showing us that. How did you even see that?"

I started to laugh, and I said, "Actually, I think my brother showed it to me." And I walked away, wiping my tear off my cheek as they gazed at the wonder of this unusual sight.

Everyone I stopped all saw the rainbow.

Up and down the sidewalk, everyone was sharing with their friends and family what they could see. Some were even trying to take pictures of it. It had actually started to kind of cause a commotion with everyone checking it out and sharing it with one another. I smiled as I heard them up and down the boardwalk. These mountains have many gifts, and I was happy to share this one.

At one point, I stopped next to a huge aspen tree, hugged it, and started to cry. It was a good cry, a cleansing cry, and even among all those people around me, it felt like a very private cry. I felt like the aspen was hugging me back. I felt like I had arms around me.

I started to walk back to my car, still hearing people telling one another about the rainbow in the sky. I even had someone ask me if I had seen it.

I smiled and said, "Yes, it's quite beautiful, isn't it?"

I then caught something to the side of my eye that made me gasp. I looked down the path, and crossing the street was a man who looked exactly like my brother.

My brother had a signature look. He always had on a dew rag on his head with a baseball hat on backward. He always wore a T-shirt with a tough-looking image on it—of course, lots of wolves, Harley Davidson T's, Huskers with cool designs, crosses, skulls, lightning, that kind of stuff. And he always wore jeans. This man walking across the street and toward me had all of that: the dew rag and baseball hat backward and a grey Harley T-shirt with mountains, lightning, and a monster riding a motorcycle. He even had jeans on, and this man was very skinny. My brother always had long thin legs, which got very thin at the end of his life. We called him frog when we were younger, remember?

This man coming toward me was the very image of my brother, and he was walking right at me like we knew each other.

I stared at him with a gaping mouth and a look of shock, I am sure, on my face.

As he got closer, I realized his face was not the same as my brother's. He looked less and less like him as he got closer.

But he had his generous, sweet smile, and as he got closer he said, "Hi. What's going on over here?"

It was as if I was in charge of all the buzz going on up and down the boardwalk.

I mean, I was, but how did he know and why did he come straight up to me like we were old friends, smiling at me?

I could not find words for a second and obviously looked like a frozen idiot because the couple of people who were with him walked right by like they were questioning why he had asked me what was going on. I did not even know how to talk evidently.

I eventually found my breath and voice again, and said to him, "Do you want to hear something crazy?"

He laughed and said, "Absolutely, I live for that!"

I told him that he was the very image of my brother and that was why I was kind of dumbstruck when he walked over.

"My brother died almost a year ago, and seeing you really surprised me, made me do a double take."

He told me he was sorry for my loss and that maybe that was why he came over. "I believe everything happens for a reason," he said. We were of the same spirit, it seemed.

"In answer to your question, yes, I do know what everyone is looking at," I confessed. Then I told him to look at the sun with his shades on and block out the sun. He did and saw the rainbow.

"Can I tell you another random thing?" I asked.

"Sure," he said.

I told him that the next day was Mark's birthday and that I was going to spread his ashes in the mountains for him. I do not really know why I told this stranger that. I just wanted to tell someone again, I think. I still had a lot of pride for my brother and liked to say his name and talk about him every chance I got.

He told me it was a really cool thing I was doing and that he was sure my brother would be with me every step I took. Then he asked how I saw this rainbow to begin with. I told him about the hawk and seeing it then. I told him that I think my brother sent the hawk to show me.

He believed I was correct and even said, "I think your brother was sending you a message with the rainbow. In fact, I guess he was sending you two messages since there are two rainbows."

It was then that I said I had just lost my dad several months before.

After offering more condolences, he asked what everyone would ask: how I was getting through it all. He said, "Well, there you go. I guess your dad had something to say too."

"I guess so." I laughed. He usually did.

I confessed again how crazy it was how much he dressed and resembled Mark. I said, "Right down to the dew rag and hat." It was then that I found out his name: Bruce. We exchanged names and hometowns. His was Kansas City. He told me he usually did not wear a hat with his dew rag but had decided to that day to keep the sun out of his face if he needed to. He took the hat off and turned it around, and it was a Nebraska Cornhusker hat.

Surprised again, I asked, "Do you like the Huskers? They were my brother's favorite team too."

"No, actually I don't. I just grabbed my nephew's hat before leaving our room, and this is the one he had," he said. He looked me in the eye then as it all started to dawn on him. Then he said, "Okay, this is officially freaky now."

I agreed!

Bruce wished me luck the next day and told me to be safe before giving me a hug and whispering, "You can do it. You are a strong lady, I can tell. And you won't be alone."

Officially freaky, indeed!

I walked back to my car, smiling, going over what had just happened in my head while still hearing people telling others to check out the rainbows around the sun. I felt the tears coming on more and more every step closer to the car I got. Once inside, I cried hard.

What had just happened? It was supposed to be just another stop for a quick look at the view. Now here I was again, wondering what kind of spiritual adventure I was on. In some ways, it felt out of my control, like something else was in charge. But it was safe still, and I was not scared, just kind of in awe. I reflected on the day and how full it was, how nourishing it was to me. I felt I had gotten everything I had wanted out of this day.

I started back to my room, and the thought came to me that I wanted to see bighorn sheep. That was the one thing I still had not seen, and this seemed like the day it might happen. So I started to look everywhere, up and down every mountainside I could see, looking for sheep.

It was always Mark who was the one in the family who spotted the wildlife on our vacations. He had a certain sense for it that just came naturally. I often would think I saw something only to have him correct me and say, "No, that's a rock."

Or a tree. Or a shadow.

We often laughed at the "sheep rocks" I would spot on our trips together to the mountains. I would get so excited and start yelling "Sheep! Sheep!" until we got closer than my brother would yell, "Rock! Rock!"

I drove on, determined to see the big horns. I got to the area called Horseshoe Park, where they are often seen and bam! There were some coming down from the mountains to drink from the lake and lick the salt off the rocks. Right on cue!

There was a ranger there who was trying to control the traffic so they could cross the road and keep the overzealous tourists from getting too close to them. I got out of my car and decided to sit in an area that would be close but not intimidating to the sheep as they crossed.

There was some excited man who was getting way too close to try to get a picture, so I yelled at him to keep his distance and not to disturb them.

My park, remember?

The park ranger heard me and came over to escort the man back to a safe distance. Then she looked at me and said, "Can you help me keep everyone back so they can cross? It looks like seven total sheep, and some of them are young and skittish."

"Sure, it would be my pleasure," I said.

So look out, everyone. I was in charge of this part of the road, and I took my job very seriously.

I set up myself close to where they were going to cross and told everyone to stay behind me. If they tried to get closer, I would tell them to back off and let them cross, and the people would. How I ended up in charge, I still am not sure. It was awesome though! I had one side of the road and the ranger had the other side—the two-woman barricade.

The sheep made their way down the mountainside, and one by one, they crossed the road down to the meadow and lake. I was ten feet away from them as they crossed at times. I felt the trust they had in me, and they knew I would protect them from all the humans watching them.

I smiled as they went by, and one stopped in the road and looked at me, maybe twenty feet away, just standing there and looking at me while some of the younger ones crossed behind it. We were eye to eye. I got chills, and I was very emotional about the animal. I said quietly, "You're welcome."

Then it made its way down with the rest of the herd and started its nightly routine.

After the sheep crossed, the cars started to move on. Others came to take pictures of the sheep in the meadow. It was an amazing sight to see, and I understood everyone's excitement, but they demanded respect as well. The park ranger came over to me and thanked me for my help. I told her it was my honor and a secret dream of mine to work in my mountains.

I laughed and said, "Are you hiring?"

I sat on a rock and watched the sun dip below the peaks and the sheep feeding and drinking and being sheep. As I sat there, I wondered at how I had done it. I had been wanting to see sheep on my way back to the room, and it had happened. Real sheep, not rocks. I marveled at how perfect my day seemed to have turned out.

I went and got a pizza from a local pizzeria and took it back to eat in the cabin. I watched some television and tried to have a sense of normality in spite of how surreal this whole day had seemed.

When it was dark out, I walked down to the creek and sat in the moonlight. I looked up in the star-filled mountain sky and drank in nature's beauty, even at night. So many stars and such deep darkness. I listened to the creek as it flowed by, and it seemed to be so mysterious in the dark, just hints of the rippling water as the moon lit it up from time to time.

I prayed in view of that heavenly sky for strength. I prayed for the power to do the next day what I came all this way to do. I asked the heavens to bless me with good weather and for the spirits of the Rocky Mountains to protect me in this most important task.

I breathed deep the mountain air and drew in all I could from that environment to help make me ready and relieve some of the nagging stress and fear about the mission I was on. I had been given so many signs that what I was doing was the right thing, but that did not make it easy. It was still the most challenging thing in my life that I was doing, even if it was the most rewarding when I was done.

Today was full of miracles and signs. I went up to the top of the mountains ...felt empowered! Saw a rainbow around the sun, I told strangers about my loss, they said things that blew me away. I ended the day by escorting mountain goats across the road to join their herd! A glorious day! I scrubbed my soul at 12,000 feet and was given moments of nourishing nature. These mountains never disappoint. A blessed day!

I went to bed that night, not expecting to sleep at all from the nerves and the never-ending thoughts. I did sleep, eventually. I did not dream that I remember.

I woke up well before the alarm that I had set at 6:00 a.m., and I felt refreshed. I felt ready, or at least as ready as I was going to get. So I got up and got going, which was easy, as I had packed everything I would need the night before. I just needed to wash my face, get dressed, and grab my things for the car and cooler.

I double-checked to make sure "Mark" and "Dad" were in my backpack, where I left them last night. I packed the car in the morning dark and got behind the wheel.

"Happy birthday, Mark," I said to myself.

I swallowed hard to hold back the emotion but was unsuccessful. I was on the road and heading for the trailhead, tears in my eyes and falling down my face. What did this day have planned for me? After the perfection of the day before, I wondered, what was this most important and sacred day going to play out like?

I drove to Bear Lake and was in the parking lot by 6:30 a.m.

This was it, the moment I had come far away to do.

I walked fast and full of purpose. This early in the morning, there were very little people and less than twenty cars. By the time I came back from the hike, the large parking lot would be full with the shuttles in full rotation. But not right now, I felt like I had the mountains all to myself, exactly the way I love it! The morning light was just starting to push the dark away, and it glowed with such an ethereal golden light that it made me stop and stare. It gave me every indication that it was going to be another glorious day!

The hike to Lake Haiyaha (Hiyayayaya) is a 3.7-mile round trip hike that starts at Bear Lake. Remember, when you plan that trip to Rocky Mountain National Park, Colorado, I told you to take, Bear Lake is a perfect stop. There are many trails leading from the lake at all different skill levels. This particular trail is nestled between Hallet Peak at 12,713 feet above sea level and Longs Peak, touching the sky at 14,259 feet. Once you reach Lake Haiyaha, you will be at 10,220 feet above sea level and above the tree line. And you will have some of the most amazing views on the planet.

I took my walking stick out of the car, put on my gloves and my jacket (it was very chilly still this early), and grabbed my backpack. I had on clothing layers for any kind of weather and plenty of water and liquids. I said good morning to the few early risers milling about and the park rangers at their station and hit the trail. And I hit it hard. I do not think I have ever done a hike with so much intensity in me as I did this morning. I was on a mission indeed, and anyone passing me would see it. Funny thing was, I did not see anyone yet. I was first on the trail for sure.

This hike is gorgeous. There are picture-perfect views around every corner, and the trail itself looks like it is in a magical forest. The smells of the pine and aspen are overwhelming. It is colorful and fresh and is a sensory overload. You do not get more "in the mountains" than this hike. I barely noticed all that. I walked hard and fast and only stopped when I needed to. I only stopped to drink water, rest myself, and catch my breath. The backpack with "Mark and Dad" in it seemed very heavy, and I was acutely aware of the contents and what I was about to do. Every step seemed to add more weight to the situation and seriousness of the action.

The first stop was at Nymph Lake. It is a little pond full of ducks and lily pads and frogs and is really sparklingly beautiful.

There is a huge old fossilized tree base on one side. This is the very place where I posed with my sister, Sandy; my niece Angie;

and two brothers Dan and Mark when we took this trail so many years ago. This is the exact spot that "Sven" took that picture of us. The legend of my love from Sweden and all the teasing that followed started right here. I sat on that piece of petrified wood and remembered what a great day it was. It was one of those perfect days that should never end, but dang it, they have to. Being in that spot for long was difficult with the thoughts of what I was doing and the fact that it was Marks birthday running through my head. I continued on before someone showed up. Still alone and grateful for that fact.

The next stop is Dream Lake and it's a bigger lake and so clear and blue that it is dreamlike. The dark green of the trees around it are such a stark contrast to the deep-blue lake that is full of moose-loving grasses and lilies. The algae from these grasses ranges from dark green to fluorescent in the sunlight. It is a really great lake to draw or paint; it is very colorful. I had a quick breakfast bar and drink here. I knew the trail would start to get steeper after this stop. But soon I was on the move again.

I climbed higher and higher into the forest and up the mountain. Every once in a while, the trees would clear an area for you to stop and get a grand view that you normally only saw in calendars, postcards, or art. It's a view that your mind enjoys but, at the same time, can hardly grasp the wonder that it is seeing and take it all in. I could see the lakes I just walked by far below me and knew I would continue to climb into the sky and they would appear even smaller at stops along the way.

One of the spectacular views on the hike
to Lake Haiyaha, Colorado.

I stopped in this one particular spot that has the most incredible view into the valley and was just awe-inspiring with the sun coming up.

I heard echoes of my brother's voice in my head. I remembered that the last time I stood on that rock, looking at the view, my brother was next to me.

Wow! It's all I could say, and that phrase was uttered many times in the hours to come.

I tried to take a picture of the sun coming up, but my phone camera would not take a picture. I would aim, hit the button, and it would just go back to the home screen. No picture taken. It was odd, and I just thought my phone was being stupid like technology sometimes is. I turned my phone off and turned it back on a few minutes later, hoping a reboot would remind it of who was in charge. But when I tried to take a picture again, it did the same thing. So much for me being in charge.

Looking back, I think I know who was in charge that day.

I continued on my hike, and still I had not seen one person. That is one huge advantage of hitting the trails so early, but it still seemed odd. I should have crossed someone else by now, especially at the lakes below. They were a very popular stop for everyone.

It felt otherworldly, like I was in my own time and space. It felt peaceful and somehow holy. I came all this way to be alone. This, of all the times on this trip, is truly when I should be alone. I did not question it but logged it in my brain as odd, same as the camera and its sudden inability to work.

I kept hiking on and tried to relax and enjoy the experience; it seemed important I remember it all: every sound and sight, all the smells that drifted in and out of my nose, how the sun filtered through trees. I felt like I was looking for a sign. I needed to see something to make me feel like Mark and Dad were with me.

But so far, nothing. I scanned the sky, looking for hawks. I looked at all the few clouds I saw, looking for a shape. I was alone, and I was in the middle of the Rocky Mountains with me, myself, my thoughts, and my mission. I could not have felt like more of a speck of water in the sea of life than I did right then. But at the same time, it felt like everything seemed far away and dreamlike. I questioned if it was all real at times. I know, freaky, but I was just having a hard time absorbing all that was taking place and the rest of what was getting ready to happen.

Let's face it. I was overwhelmed by what I was going through, by what I was getting ready to do. I didn't feel real at the time, and I almost felt "floaty," if that makes sense. That is why I am convinced I cruised so fast up the mountain and got to the lake before the rest of the world; it was because I was floating, maybe riding on angels' wings.

Don't get me wrong. The hike was amazing, and every break I took was a feast to my mind, eyes, and soul. I climbed up a couple times on rocks and waited for a hiker to spy on—you know, the way

I like to, mountain lion style. But nobody ever walked by. No hikers had been seen or heard since I left the area right above Bear Lake. Looking back, I can never remember being on a trail all alone in all the times I had been in these mountains. You eventually will run into someone along the way.

The closest to this kind of seclusion I have had before this was when I was on Bierstadt Trail in the late fall.

It was in October sometime, and I only crossed two hikers on the way up and then saw one man at the lake when I arrived. He left as soon as it started to snow, and I sat on a rock, eating my lunch in the soft, quiet mountain snow with the partially frozen lake in front of me. It was so silent you could feel the weight of it and actually hear the snowflakes hit the trees, rocks, and me. I sat there with my hoodie up, gloves and winter gear on, munching on my sandwich. I remember the rock with the shape of me in snow and my legs dangling when I jumped off it to go.

I did cross a bear coming up that trail on that hike, so animals but very few humans. It was a nerve-racking experience, crossing a bear on a hike. He came down the mountain vertically as I was on a trail horizontally. We eyed each other about thirty yards away from each other. He stood on his hind legs, sniffed the air, then moved along. It was a tense but invigorating moment.

But on this hike, zilch! Not one human or animal for that matter. As I said, not that I am complaining. I got to the point where I knew I was super close. There is a wood bridge over the runoff water that comes down the mountain that I knew was one of the last places to stop before getting to the lake.

I stopped there and stood on that little rustic bridge. I stood there, feeling the morning sun finally warming up the enormous sky. I listened to the water babble below me, always so close to a word that I strained my ears so I wouldn't miss it. Every nerve in my body was on edge and ready to snap. Now I desperately wanted to see someone, anyone, just to prove to myself that this was real. I was afraid I was dreaming it all and I would have to wake up and start the day all over again.

When I felt the strength to move on to the final push, I slowly walked off that bridge. My feet felt like lead, and the tears were just below the surface. I had thought about this for so long that it was like when you are opening your presents at Christmas or your birthday. You have looked forward to a moment or even dreaded a moment or just thought about a moment for so long that when it is actually here and now, it seems hard to believe.

But I was here, and I was ready. Did I have a choice? I had come all this way. I could not back out now.

With one step in front of the other, I moved toward the lake, floated maybe even at times. I was trying very hard to stay in the moment and enjoy what I was doing, to not let the thoughts and doubt creep in and cloud my memory, to not be overtaken by my own loss and grief, to be strong.

I got to the lake, which is a clear azure mountain lake with those amazing peaks jutting out of the water. The rocks around it are all in different sizes, from small loose ones to boulders the size of cars and buses. I climbed over a few of those and got to a spot that was in the perfect view of the lake with the highest peaks in the background.

I stood there, breathing very deeply the thin cold air with the sun on my face. I stared at all the beauty around me, which literally took my breath away. It was a perfect day, ridiculously faultless blue mountain sky with just the right amount of high white clouds drifting by.

The lake was below me, nestled between rocks and crevices, and I stepped out closer to the big water on a rock there. There was room to spread the ashes and plenty of rocks to hide my mini baggies with the precious hair, ashes, images, and words to both my dad and my brother. This was the perfect place to honor them, where I wanted to leave pieces of them, pieces that could stay in this gorgeous place forever and let nature claim again.

I decided that since it was Mark's birthday and I was spreading his actual ashes with Alpine's hair, I would release a part of my dad first. I fooled myself into thinking that that would be easier than

Mark and a way to ease into the thought and the actual action of spreading Mark's ashes.

What a dumb idea.

You see, I was very fragile at this point. This was my "strength" trip, remember? But until that exact moment, I had not realized how fragile I really was.

The fact that I was still in shock from my dad's last breath just eighty-seven days ago (or only two months and twenty-six days ago) really did not crack into my thoughts until then. It seemed that my mind was really unable to commit to admitting that he was really gone.

I was in the denial part of that particular grief.

And I guess that's the point that I ultimately hope helps someone reading this story—that grief for each person is different and it is all correct. There is no right or wrong way to grieve, and grieving within yourself is different for each death. We don't grieve the loss of a pet or friend the way we do a parent or sibling. It is different for each person.

At this particular point, I really was not even dealing with the fact that my dad was gone. How could I?

I was still trying to heal from losing my brother in such a long, nasty way. And the fact that I was in full-out denial did not even register in me until that exact moment.

So I took my dad's mini baggie out of the backpack and placed the velvet bag with Mark inside down on the rock next to my backpack.

I did my best to say some kind words and tell my dad how much I loved and missed him. And I opened his mini bag and sprinkled some of the confetti into the lake and let one of the fake diamonds fall in the water. Then I tucked the baggie into a rock crevice near the water where it would be safe. It would take a lot to move it. I kissed it before I did so he would always know how much he meant to me.

And then I cried and cried.

I looked around and decided that before I spread Mark's ashes, I would take a picture so I could show my family where I had left them. How amazing this lake and mountains are.

Again, my camera refused to work. It would bring up the camera, I would hit the take-a-picture button, and back to home screen it went—just like before. I could not believe it.

It had been working fine all trip, all month, all year. Then it decides not to work at this exact moment. I blamed it on the altitude, which even my mind was telling me was a lie since I took pictures at higher altitude the day before.

Looking back, it seems the moment was just too sacred, too precious to humanize with photos. I am relieved it was unable to be photographed. It would have changed the memory of it somehow. It would be less magical.

Frustrated, I decided it just was not meant to be and now it was time to spread Mark's ashes while I still had the strength to do so.

I took his baggie off the rock and read out loud the words I had written on it. I looked around to make sure I was alone, and boy, was I ever. I still had not seen one person since the hike started, and I decide that was okay since I was making a spectacle of myself with all my crying and carrying on.

So as I said, I took out the baggie, read the words written on it, wished him a happy birthday, and told him I missed and loved him and that Alpine did too but that he was doing okay and getting more spoiled than I would ever admit to him.

But I was sure he saw how we gave him lots of hugs and treats and people food, which was a huge no-no with my brother. In fact, the first couple of times we gave Al a plate to lick or people food, he had such a guilty look on his face. But he was my brother's caregiver in the end, and he deserved every moment of happiness we could give him.

I told Mark that I was spreading part of Alpine, his mountain dog, with him so they could still be together and Alpine could protect him always. I knew he approved of that because Alpine was his boy, his last responsibility when he left this earth, and he loved him like the family that he is.

So in my mind, the thought of how it was all going to happen had played itself out hundreds of times. I pictured me saying all the right words because I said them in all my rehearsals perfectly. I pictured myself opening the mini Ziploc with Mark's precious ashes and grandly scattering them into the wind as it was lifted away on the mountain current and flew into the sky and up toward the heavens. I could almost hear the angels singing.

SCREECH! So now let me give you the reality version, although—do not get me wrong—admittedly pretty amazing but still reality.

I opened my brother Mark's baggie containing his ashes and part of Alpine's hair that I cut off his chest. I took the baggie and started to sprinkle the contents into the lake. Right as I started to release the ashes, a wind came up and blew the ashes back to me.

I had ashes on my sweatshirt, shorts, and cheek.

I know what you are thinking. Eeeewwww! That is gross! I have to admit—at first, I was like "Ahhhhh … what just happened?"

But then I started to laugh because in that instant, I heard Mark's voice in my head, clear as a bell, saying, "One last hug! One last kiss on your cheek!" That rascal had made the wind come up and blow those ashes back at me. I was sure of it.

There was no breeze toward me now. It had just happened for an instant.

So I brushed them off and blew a kiss back to Mark, and in my mind, I told him how naughty he was for doing that, although I was smiling at the macabre humor. Hey, I read Stephen King and enjoy all things horror, so it really was not as bad as it might have been for other people. Plus, it is my brother, and we share the same blood and DNA.

So through many tears and trying to say kind words but overwhelmed and unable to speak, I sprinkled the rest of his ashes and Alpine's hair into the lake. I watched them sink and Al's hair drift off a little before going under. I watched some of the lighter ashes float into the rocks surrounding the mountain lake or disappearing in the wind. I tucked his little mini bag into an area of rocks by my Dad's bag. I looked around and let the breeze blow over the tears on my cheeks, turning some of them into little icicles.

I stood on the big rock above where I had just tucked the two men I loved and missed so much, even if just a representative of them, in a symbolic goodbye to them in my own way.

As I stood there, I howled …and howled …and howled!

I howled for Mark, I howled for me, and I howled that my dad's spirit was now running free and knew all his pain was gone. I wanted Mark's free soul to hear me and know his pack would always be there for him and we could not wait to see him again. I howled to free myself and my pent-up grief and to be the true spiritual mountain girl I was!

Aawwwwwwoo!

Then I stood on that rock, facing those majestic peaks, and I tried—I mean I really tried—to sing Mark "Happy Birthday." I would start to sing, break down, try to start over, break down, try to continue from where I stopped, and break down. But I had to finish it! It was his birthday, and I had to find the inner strength to do this. The spreading of the ashes and trip up had started to catch up with me emotionally, and I could not keep it together. I was seriously struggling in that moment.

I stood there with my head hung down, weeping and feeling so alone and worn out emotionally. I had done it, but it was not done yet. *Laurie, keep it together,* I kept telling myself.

That was when I heard it.

"Good morning." It was said in the most pleasant voice I remember hearing.

I turned around and saw a man. Okay, you are going to think I am crazy for just a few minutes here, but I swear all I am going to say is true.

This man looked like the Jesus I grew up seeing in all my CCD classes, in all the art I have ever seen of Jesus. This was the man. He had silky long dark hair under a fisherman's hat. He had a silky brown beard and the kindest blue eyes I could ever remember looking into. He was dressed like he was going fishing—with cargo shorts and hiking boots. *Jesus in hiking gear* is what came into my mind.

The perfect disguise.

As I stared at him with a look of shock on my face, he asked me, "Can I come out to that rock with you?"

I finally closed my mouth and found my voice and said, "Yeah, of course." And I wiped my eyes and face full of tears before he came closer.

As he climbed on to the rock, I asked, "Where did you come from?"

Dumb shocked! Because it seemed he had literally just come from nowhere. I didn't hear him coming or notice him before he spoke.

He said, "I am lost. I was supposed to meet some friends to fish at a lake with an H in it. And I think this is the lake, but I don't know where my friends are."

"Well, this is Lake Haiyaha, so you are in the right place," I said. As he just stood there, smiling at me, I asked again, "I mean, where did you come from? I have not seen anyone all morning."

He just smiled and repeated what he had said about being lost and looking for his friends. Then he introduced himself. "I am Nicholas. Nick."

And I told him my name. Just Laurie.

He asked if I was okay, noting that he could tell I had been crying. I told him, "Are you ready for your random story of the day?"

And then I proceeded to tell him what I had just done, that I had spread Mark's ashes and Dad's items, that when he walked up, I was trying to sing "Happy Birthday" to Mark.

I followed that with another "Where did you come from?"

The fact that he just showed up right then and there was blowing my mind. The fact that he looked like God's Son was freaking me out a little too.

He ignored the question I had already asked him three times now, and he said, "Well, we need to sing 'Happy Birthday' to him then. What is his name again?"

I remember noticing that he said *is* instead of *was*. I thought that was beautiful.

Then in the clearest, purest voice, he sung loud and grandly, "Happy birthday to you. Happy birthday to you. Happy birthday, dearest Mark. Happy birthday to you!"

I just stood there, completely unable to say a thing or squeak out one note. I just stood there, overwhelmed by the fact that this was all happening. I just stood there, listening to this man sing Mark "Happy Birthday." Then I broke down.

He had shown up right when I needed him and was a stranger, yet he felt like someone I knew.

He then asked me if I was all right.

I lied and told him I was fine, and I thanked him for singing to my brother for me, that I just could not do it and that his timing was perfect.

Then he asked me a question I was not expecting. He asked if he could pray with me.

Stunned, I said, "Of course, I would love it if you would pray with me."

This stranger was being so genuine that I could feel it in my heart that his kindness was warming my soul. Somehow, I was very aware that not only did he care about me but that he loved me. And I strangely felt love for him. It made no sense, and there was not a single inkling of sexual attraction. It was much deeper than that. I loved him because I knew he loved me. Does that make sense?

This stranger named Nicholas, Nick, held my hands, standing on that mountain rock under some of the most powerful peaks that Mother Nature has to offer, and prayed with me. He said things that blew my mind as if he had known me and my family all his life. I just stood there, weeping and unable to understand how he was saying these things.

I am giving you the short version and summarizing, but he said things like this:

> Thank you, Father, for giving Laurie the strength to make this difficult but important journey and calming all her doubts and showing her that she is strong enough to do this.
>
> And although she misses her own father very much, she knows that he is with you and Mark, home again, and that he is not in the pain that he had to endure for those last years of his life.
>
> We are humbled by what Laurie is doing for her brother today, on his most important first birthday away from the ones he left behind. He was a fighter and held on tight to life and deserves to be honored.
>
> Continue to show Laurie the faith she will need to continue on and begin to heal from today. Please give her loved ones, Mark and her father, the power to show her that she is not alone and that they miss and continue to love her as well in your kingdom.

You can only imagine the look on my face as he said all this. It was all private, and it was all true. And how on earth did he know?

Now let me tell you something. I did not tell this stranger about my dad and his struggles, only that he had died six months after my brother. I don't even remember telling him that Mark died of cancer, much less that he fought it as long as he did.

I know I didn't tell him it was our first birthday without him. And he directly addressed the signs I had been seeing.

It was crazy, and I stood there, trembling, because I was so grateful that he was there, saying all the right things when I physically was unable to.

After he said these things, I stared at him again as he smiled that loving, caring smile, and I asked again, laughing, maybe even a bit uncomfortably, "Where did you come from?" My brain was trying to understand.

He got serious and said, "Let us pray." And then he started to recite the Lord's Prayer with me.

"Our Father, who art in heaven, hallowed be thy name, thy kingdom come, thy will be done …"

After reciting the Lord's Prayer, he hugged me. And I collapsed with grief. He held me up, this stranger from nowhere. He made me stand up and stand up strong.

We stood there for a moment, looking at the mountains, and then he asked if I was okay. I told him I was, and he said he was going to look for his friends.

But he said to me, "If you need me, though, just call for me. It doesn't matter where I am. I will hear you, and I will find you. You sure you are okay?"

I told him I was and thanked him for being so kind.

He walked away then and headed toward the tree trail around the lake. I watched him going away, and I felt so sad that he was leaving. I wished he could stay with me and help me more. I remember the feeling of dread that he was leaving, feeling lost without him. I watched him until I could not see him anymore.

I sat down on the rock then and grabbed something to drink. I was trying really hard to process what just happened. Did a stranger who suspiciously looked like Jesus just give a mountain eulogy for my dad and brother? Did he just show up out of nowhere when I was at my most hopeless and scared?

Seriously, what just happened?

I felt so anguished, more alone, and in despair than at any time in my life. I sat down on the rock and wept—full-body weeping and racking sobs. I cried and cried and sobbed and sobbed. I looked around and saw nobody and cried out loud, echoing off the water and peaks, desperate cries from a beaten-down brokenhearted woman.

Then I sat there and desperately tried to get it together. As I wiped my tears and tried to compose myself, I realized I still needed to get back down this mountain. My hike was only half over. There was no ranger around to pull me off the mountain. I had climbed to the top, and now I had to climb back down. It felt like an impossible task.

"Get it together, girl," I kept saying to myself. "Deep breaths. You can do this." This was my pep talk in between sobs. I was a mess!

Just when I started to doubt I would ever have the power to even move away from the rock I was sitting on, I heard another voice.

"Hello down there. Need some company?"

I turned around and saw a very attractive young man. He was blond and clear-eyed and handsome. I said, "Sure, come on down." I was laughing in a self-conscious, embarrassed way. As he got closer, I noticed that he was even more beautiful, and I noticed he was probably from Denmark, Sweden, or some Scandinavian area. As he came down, talking, I noticed his accent. Definitely European.

I tried to clean up a little and get myself together. I mean, here was this gorgeous creature. I could not be a mess in front of him. He asked me if I was okay, and I laughed and said, "Well, I think I will be."

He smiled in answer and said, "Good."

Then he stood there in full glory of the mountains and their strength, and he said, "Look at this place. It is so beautiful here. This could be heaven."

I drew in my breath in shock, looking at him, and could not believe what I had just heard him say—a heaven reference from another stranger. What was going on here?

I said, "Well, it's funny you say that. If you would like a good story to tell your friends ..." And I continued to tell him the general reason that I was there.

He said that he thought that it was really incredible what I had just done, and he hoped someone would do something amazing for him when he died.

He then introduced himself, and as I stood there, locking my knees against the possibility that he was going to say "Sven." He said, "Andrew. Andy."

Again, with the formal name first and then his shorter name. Very weird.

I introduced myself and asked about his accent. Where was he from?

Then he said it, "Sweden."

I laughed so hard I almost fell down.

He grabbed my arm, looking at me with this knowing look, starting to laugh himself.

He told me that he was in the United States to see the Rockies because he had heard so much about them. He said he had decided to do this particular hike this morning on a whim. He was glad he did because he got to hear my special story.

At that moment, Nick walked by again, going the other direction.

"You still doing okay, Laurie?" he asked.

I waved and said hello and that, yes, I was doing fine. Andy said to me then, "See, you are not so alone, are you?" And he smiled at me.

Andy and I stood there in silence for a few minutes, just taking in the scenery. He was right; it was heaven here.

Then Andy said, "Well, I better keep moving. How about you?"

I told him that actually I was feeling good and ready to start to head down.

"You going to be okay?" he asked, looking at me with seriousness in his face.

I assured him, "I'm feeling much better, thanks." Looking into those light-blue eyes, I knew that if I had asked him to stay, he would have. I had that familiar feeling of having a complete stranger caring for me.

He bounced away with his blond hair blowing in the breeze, waving and saying he was heading up still and that I should be safe the rest of my trip. I told him the same and wished him luck on his

USA adventure. As I watched him walk away, I had a deep feeling for him. I did not want him to go but was grateful that he came to me when I needed it most.

Andy from Sweden was gone, as was Nick.

I was alone again, but I felt renewed.

I took several deep breaths and actually felt strong. I felt cleansed. I felt blessed. These two strangers were why, and I thanked God for sending them to me in my hour of need. I truly did, and I 100 percent believe that they were sent to me to help me in my time of trouble. By who was the question?

I mean, ultimately, God or whatever deity you believe in intervened, but in who's behalf? Or was it just God's love I was feeling? Was he just watching over one of his flock? The word *miracle* kept jumping into my head, because I am convinced I would still be crying on that mountainside today if not for the strength those two (Angels? Saints? Jesus himself?) had given me.

Believe me, it was not lost on me that Nick is also my favorite saint. Saint Nicholas, a.k.a. Santa Claus. And I know the world is small, but to have this young man from Sweden (a.k.a. Sven 2000) just show up when I needed help …really?

I mean, come on, what are the odds? It made my head spin.

I sat there, marveling at all that had happened and smiling and laughing to myself that it was over. The laughter was relief and amazement and not appropriate for what I had just done. But the joy that I felt at that moment was tangible. I could hear it. I could taste it. I could feel it. It had been a long time, but it felt familiar.

Wow! Just wow!

As I sat there, thinking about getting up and moving again, I was desperately looking all around in every direction, hoping to see either one of these men again if even just from a distance, to prove to myself that it was all real, and it did happen. But I knew deep down inside that I would never see them—not now, maybe never again. What they had come to do was done, and now it was up to me to take care of myself again.

I could do it too. I knew I could.

I got up, grabbed my stuff, put my backpack back on and started walking around the lake. There was a different bounce in me, a lighter bounce. I took in where I was and what I was seeing again, memorizing it. I told myself that I would stay at the lake until I saw another person and then I would leave. After all I had this scene all to myself, so why not enjoy it? It is not often in this day and age that we are alone, and at a mountain lake over ten thousand feet above sea level, well, you better take advantage and embrace that.

So I climbed around and did my thing, and I sat down by the lake, looking out over the water. Then I heard a voice. No, it was not the sound of one of my kind strangers, but a lady talking to her husband about the hotel they were staying at. Then I heard some kids' voices yelling back and forth at one another. Hello, people, this is my cue to go.

So as they approached the lake, smiling and saying how beautiful it was, I walked past them, saying, "Good morning." The lady asked me if this was the end; she was exhausted. She could not go much farther.

I laughed and reminded her she still has to go down, and I said, "Yes, this is the end."

Inside my head, that phrase meant more than how she took it.

It was the end of her trail up that morning but a beginning for me. But that is one of the awesome things about private thoughts. Words can be powerful even when they are just everyday words, just like every song lyrics means something different to each person. The words we say can sometimes mean much more than they appear. We never know what anyone is thinking unless they tell us.

I walked back to the trail and started down the path. I left that divine lake and almost immediately felt like I was a new person. I passed several hikers and said hello to all I crossed. It was weird because as soon as I saw those people at the lake, I kept seeing more and more people. It was like time was frozen for me while I was doing my ceremony, if you will, and now time was back on.

My time of isolation was over, but I was okay with that. I had just had an amazing experience, and I felt like I had a secret over everyone else. I had just had this precious, magical moment but didn't have one person to share it with.

Did I even want to share it? It felt like a gift, but a very private gift. It was like I had won the lottery but could not tell anyone about it.

I walked down the trail, past all the trees and rocks, and let the sun shine on me in the tree breaks. I was really enjoying this new-found freedom from my heavy responsibility that had finally been released. Then all at once I stopped in my tracks.

It was like I had just hit a wall, sliding to a stop. I still remember the gravel noise under my boots at my halt.

I stopped completely, unable to move because a thought had finally allowed itself to come to full bloom in my stunned mind, an obvious thought to you and to me now but something I didn't really think about until that exact moment.

Yes, those two strangers were sent to me by Dad and my brother Mark.

It was as clear as that mountain sky that Dad had sent Nickolas, Nick. My dad had been there with me and was seeing that I needed help in this very spiritual mission, and he sent it. He sent it in a form I would recognize and be at ease with—Jesus from my child-hood images—and exactly when I needed it. He even had Nick say a eulogy and prayer with me. My parents are very faithful Catholics, and I am sure both have a special place in heaven for how loyal they have been to their faith. It was all the things my dad would have wanted to do if he was with me at that moment, which I know now that he was.

In my mind, I could hear my dad say, "Well, if you are going to spread Mark's ashes, you need to pray for him. Do it right and properly in our belief, even if we are not in church."

My dad loved me, but he also knew that I was in no condi-tion to pray alone. So he sent Nick to come say the right things and properly send my brother's ashes into heaven. How else would he have known all the things he did if my dad had not sent him there with the information? It just does not add up that he would appear out of nowhere and be my strength when I needed it. It was not by accident. I know this is true. I can feel it in my heart.

As for our handsome young Andrew, Andy, it was also clear to me in that moment that he was sent from Mark—yes, kind of as a joke since he was young and gorgeous and from Sweden, just like Sven was (in our minds at least). An inside joke that only I would get, even though it did feel like Andy was in on it too from the smile he gave me. I imagine my brother knowing that I needed help in that moment and some motivation to get back down the mountain. So being the brother that he is, he sent a cute boy to get me moving again.

I can almost hear him say, "Dad sent you someone to pray with. I am sending you the hot young Sweden man to show you that you are strong enough to finish this. I am here with you too." His voice echoed in my mind.

I stood there on the trail, laughing that, yes, that was exactly the plot of what had just happened. My dad knew I needed to treat this like a funeral or memorial since that really was what it was. He sent prayers and singing both, like a mass. And Mark knew I would appreciate and sober up my sobbing in front of this young man, the man who said it looked like heaven to him, a man whom I could drain some energy from. He was so full of life. And that was what he did—he refueled me.

As I stood on that path, I leaned against a pine tree because my knees had started to shake. All at once, I wanted to tell everyone what had just happened.

I was crying and laughing at the same time, filled with love and relief and mostly belief. It was overwhelming when it came pounding into my self-conscious the way it did. It took me a moment to collect myself.

Wow! That just happened!

I still could not really believe it and could not wait to tell my mom about it, to tell my whole family about it.

Wow!

Would they believe me? Would I believe me?

It was crazy, but I knew what had just happened was real and sacred. I was not reading something into nothing. I knew that. And I did not care one bit if anyone ever believed me because I knew the truth. The truth is that we are never alone when it comes to our deceased loved ones. They are still with us and can still guide us. They can help us and show us the way in a loving, gentle way.

Because they are love.

All the earthly burdens and stresses are gone from them now. They want nothing but love and peace for us too. It went from that belief of such a notion to full out knowing that it is true. That morning changed my life on many levels. I was touched by all of them, spiritually, emotionally, and physically. I would never be the same.

I am grateful that I changed that day. I still have my anxiety and pressure just like everyone else, but I have a small fire in me now that comforts me, knowing that I will see my dad again. I will hug my brother someday. I will.

When I could finally stop saying "Wow!" to myself and my legs felt like they could hold my body again, I headed back down the trail. I was speaking to both of them in my mind and out loud, mostly thanking them for the aid they sent, telling them I missed them and could not wait to see them again someday. I spoke to them as if they were right next to me because I felt like they were. I swear I even felt them hold my hand at times.

The hike down was much less intense emotionally and physically than the hike up to the lake. As I said, the burden of spreading the ashes had been lifted. I felt like I had done good by Mark and that both he and my dad were proud of me. I was proud of myself. This was a huge thing to tackle and to tackle alone, so I felt very good about where I was in my life at that exact moment.

Lake Haiyaha, Rocky Mountain National Park, Colorado

Since the hike down was more casual, without the sense of urgency that I had before, I made more stops. I stopped many times to enjoy the spectacular views and to just chill and reflect. It felt good, and the weather was perfect, so why not? I was in no hurry now. Going down takes about half the time of going up, so I knew I could slow myself down a little. Plus, my backpack felt about twenty pounds lighter without the ashes and pouches in it.

On one stop down, there is a runoff area where there had been enough snow left to create a good-size waterfall. It has rock ledges along the way and a great view of the lakes below. The trees frame it so perfectly that it is a must-stop camera opportunity. I did not bother with the camera. I knew it would misbehave again. But I did climb down the ravine and sit on a ledge overlooking the scene.

There was a man on the trail above that had stopped and was taking a picture, and I asked him if he wanted me to move to get out of his picture. He asked if he could come down to the ledge instead.

I told him to come down; it would be an amazing shot from where I was. He climbed down the ravine and sat on the rock with me.

We marveled at how pretty it was. He told me that he was from the Midwest. I told him, "Me too." He was from Missouri but loved the Rocky Mountains. I told him I was from Nebraska but loved the mountains as well. We introduced ourselves and shared that we were both mountain hiking alone. We agreed that the best way to hike is alone. We sat listening to the water.

He asked me if I was camping. I laughed and said, "No, I am not that much of a mountain girl anymore. I prefer a bed and hot shower." He laughed and said he understood. I then asked him if he knew what time it was.

He looked at his watch and said, "It's 11:11."

I stared at him and said, "Are you sure?"

You see, 11:11 are numbers that have always meant to me that they were numbers from the universe, telling you are on the right path. They are numbers of God. Any double numbers are a good sign: 22, 33, 44 …etc. It was at least what I was always told and thought spiritually. To hear those numbers now was comforting.

I started to laugh, and this stranger asked, "What?"

I told him what I was musing about. And he actually said, he had heard the same theory too. Feeling some kind of kinship with this stranger, I began. I could not help myself.

I sat on this rock with this new arrival and told him everything that had just happened. I think I was so ready to tell somebody, anybody, that I just unleashed. I edited myself a little on the spiritual stuff but told him about the promise and how I had just spread Mark's ashes and pieces of Dad's memory at the lake.

I did not tell him about Nick or Andy. I was still having some doubts that they were really there. It still sounded a little crazy to me, to be honest.

He was a good audience, and he listened intently. He only interrupted me once to tell me, "Yes! Yes, I have that in my will—to have my ashes spread up here at Emerald Lake!"

Then he really got interested in the story. He hung on my every word and had a gleam in his eyes, mumbling "Perfect" and "Oh my god" from time to time.

After telling him everything, he sat there staring at the crashing mountain water with me and said, "That is a great story and an amazing thing that you did for your brother. He would be so proud of you. I am, and I am not even your brother. I would be proud if you were my sister—I mean it."

This brought tears to my eyes.

He then got really serious with me. "Thank you. I mean really, thank you for telling me what you did today. I told you I have that in my will, but until now, I never really thought about who would actually do it for me. I mean, logistically, who would do what you just did for me when I die?" He then said, "I am going to talk to my sister when I get back. I mean, otherwise, who will do it? My lawyer? My parents can't. I am not married. No real other family."

He sat in silence as I let him think.

He finally said, "You just never know, and I want to have it done special, like you just did, by someone who loves me—not my lawyer or a stranger. I am going to make her promise me."

He told me how privileged he felt to meet me as I held back tears and how he hoped I had a really fun time the rest of my trip. I deserved it after what I had been through. He thanked me again and said, "You really do not know how much this changes things in my life."

I laughed nervously with the start of tears overflowing from my eyes. He climbed back up the mountainside and back on to the trail and waved goodbye as he headed up to the lake, the lake that he would now see very differently.

He yelled back as he left, "It's 11:44 now, just so you know!" He was laughing and shaking his head. "How about that?"

I laughed and waved back and said to myself, *Yeah, how about that?* It was another bizarre encounter on this magical day, only this time I am the stranger who has touched another person's life. That was a good feeling.

Remember, at this time, I had not been much of a contributor to society in a long time because I had been in a grief cocoon of my own. Helping others always makes you feel better about yourself and helps to restore some self-worth. Everything—and I mean everything—happens for a reason.

Smiling and feeling satisfied, I climbed back up to the trail myself. I continued down the path, my stride strong and confident. It was such a perfect day, and I felt as close to perfect as I had since I could remember. My cadence was steady, and my walking stick was feeling light in my hand and hitting all the strong, solid rocks.

I found a private area to climb down to with another perfect view. It was a huge rock, but to get there, you had to climb down where there was some loose rock and not many trees or shrubbery to hold on to. The incline was steep, and it was scary. I remember saying "Lord, look after me on this one because it looks kind of dangerous" as I started down the unnerving side of the mountain.

I climbed down, mostly on my behind, slip sliding away, until I hit an area that I could stand up on and walk down the rest of the way to the massive boulder. I stepped on the flat, smooth rock and did a little dance!

I made it! It was my rock! I stood there with my arms raised like Rocky and jumped up and down, "Feeling strong now!" I cried out. Then I threw punch combos in the air. Jab, jab, jab, upper cut, upper cut, jab.

Pure pleasure. I was on a boulder that was at the kind of angle that you had ultimate privacy. The hikers on the path above me could not see me, nor could I see them. I could almost hear them, but the mountain wind and trembling leaves were loud enough for me not to notice. I was all alone again. I was savoring the moment.

Speaking of savoring, I decided to sit and eat my lunch. I had a breakfast bar and juice boxes, some fruit snacks earlier, but they were wearing off, and I had suddenly realized that I was starving. I took off my backpack and removed some layers of clothing and spread out on my picnic area, this mountain rock.

I got my water out and drank deeply. I looked around and also drank deeply with my eyes. There were so many colors to take in—from the moss, to the rocks, to the small trees growing around me in all different shades. As I looked at the view and felt the breeze and sun on my face, I felt at peace. I remember looking around so I could capture this moment in my mind for days in my life in the future that I would need peace. What I felt then was the epitome of it.

I reached in my backpack and got my sandwich out. I grabbed my baggie of chips and laid it on the rock along with a container that had juice in it. As I sat there, eating my lunch, I noticed a white butterfly flying around. It flew all over, stopping at every flower it could manage to and finding different trees to land on. I watched it flutter around, at times the mountain breeze controlling where it went.

Then as I sat there, chewing my chips, this beautiful white butterfly landed on my picnic rock, within under a foot away from me.

"Well, hello there. Can I help you?" was what I said. In my mind, I heard myself say, *Or can you help me?*

I laughed, ate my lunch. The whole time, this white butterfly sat on the rock in the sun or flew off, only to return and sit again on my rock. At one time, it felt so much like this butterfly was keeping an eye on me that I asked it, "Who are you?"

It was the tamest butterfly I had ever seen in the sense that it never flew more than ten feet away from me. And even when it was sitting on the rock and I was fumbling with my baggies and backpack, it stayed put. I stood up to wrap my clothes' layers around my waist or stuff them in my backpack and it sat there on the rock below. It was not threatened, just like it was waiting patiently for me to get done so we could go.

I turned and saw the climb I had in front of me to get back to the path. I forgot how dangerous it was. I felt like a cat who climbed up the tree and then could not get back down. I would like to say this is the first time I have felt this way hiking in the mountains. I would like to say that. But that is why I have a walking stick and good boots.

I climbed up the side of the mountain to the path, sometimes on my knees. It was not pretty or glamorous or looking like a beer or soda commercial in any way, but I made it. Thankful that I was still alive, I leaned against a rock and caught my breath. While I stood there, recovering, two older men walked by. They were probably in their sixties but were seasoned hikers for sure.

They stopped to ask me if I was all right. I showed them where I had just climbed to and from, my picnic rock, and they told me I was crazy. They laughed and kidded each other that twenty years ago, they would have tried it too.

They told me I was lucky I did not get hurt, and said, "You must have an angel watching over you."

Really? I thought.

As I watched them continue on their hike, I noticed my butterfly friend had returned. It fluttered around my head and almost got in my face as if to say, "What were you thinking? Be careful!"

I moved along down the trail with the butterfly lingering behind and around me, still seeming a little displeased with me.

I hiked for over a half hour, in fact, with that butterfly never leaving my side. It was the steepest part of the trail, and it was during points when you had a lot of switchbacks and the trail turned to loose rocks at points. It was hard on the knees and feet. But I still saw that butterfly. At times, it would fly in my face or around my head.

When I stopped for a drink of water once, it landed on my shirt.

"Are you serious right now?" was what I asked it as I laughed at its silliness. I was not even surprised; it was that kind of day.

Eventually, I came to the bottom of the trail; it was pretty level and even after this point. This is where you start to head back to Bear lake and past Dream and Nymph Lake. There were streams and grassland, where there was an abundance of fish and bugs as well as the occasional elk sleeping in the bush.

There is a log bridge going across all the gathered water, and I had stopped at the side I had come from to rest before going on.

That is when I saw the white butterfly sitting on a tree on the side of the path.

I approached the butterfly, admiring how truly gorgeous it was. It had little glimmering specks on it, and its body looked yellowish. I was looking very closely at it, and it did not move.

"Who are you?" I asked again.

It just stayed where it was. I even put my hand on the tree it was sitting on, and it did not even flinch.

"Well, thank you for keeping me company down the mountain, but I got it from here," I said.

It was at this time that a man with a little girl of about seven years old were walking across the bridge.

"What do you have there?" the man asked.

"Oh, I have this little butterfly that has been following me around," I told them.

In the Rockies, you always seem to see someone that has spied something that you ask about. "What do you see?" It is a normal question in the mountains. I am not sure butterfly is always the normal answer though.

The man got super excited and said, "Look, Lily, it's a butterfly!"

She squealed with delight, and I showed her where it was on the tree.

They both "ooohed" and "aawwwwed" over it and were amazed that it was not flying away.

I told the butterfly then "You have followed me long enough. Now you can start to follow Lily." She lit up at the possibility.

I started laughing, telling them to have fun, and started across the bridge. The man followed me on to it and stopped me.

"Thank you so much for showing us that butterfly. You see, they are Lily's favorite, and we have been looking for one all day," he said.

I said he was welcome and he said, "You have a blessed day!"

I said to do the same, walking away and thinking, *Mister, you have no idea!*

I continued down the familiar trail and stopped at all the places I went by too fast and distracted on the way up.

At Dream Lake, I found myself alone again. There was not even anyone sitting by the side, taking a break. So I sat down and took a rest. It was really getting warm, and the clouds had started to roll in from the west. They were white and poufy and not menacing at all, and I was grateful for them. Without the breeze they were floating on, it would have been on the verge of hot. And it was only going to get warmer as I got lower in altitude.

I sat at the edge of this beautiful lake and closed my eyes. I let anything at all pop into my mind at that time, just letting all the thoughts go and relax my mind along with my body. A remarkable thing happened.

Nothing.

For the first time since I can remember, nothing was in my mind.

I was not worried about my dad or Mark. I was not thinking about this trip. I was not thinking about work. My mind did not jump to any subject whatsoever. I heard, I smelled, I tasted. I let all my senses run amok. I had finally loosened the clench on my mind that I had been tightening for a while now. It was bliss.

My bliss was interrupted by a couple with a baby in their back-pack stopping and interrupting the quiet. Again, it was my cue to move on. But what a wonderful thing that had just happened. Aahhhh! It was all I could think. I said hello to this young couple as I cruised past with yet another personal secret.

I walked past Nymph Lake, smiling widely at the tree where "Sven" from Sweden had taken that picture so long ago. I touched it as I walked by, almost feeling for a tremor or something echoing in the wood. My senses felt so alive! Funny how life moves and flows. On to Bear Lake and the end of the road. There were always many people around this area, and today was no exception.

As I walked to my car and started to load it, I noticed the clouds moving in even farther out of the mountains, and now they were becoming a little darker. The timing of my hike seemed too perfect.

"Get off the mountain when the lightning and weather roll in" is always the best rule.

After hitting the portable potties, I hit the road, winding my car back down the hillside. The dark clouds seem to follow me the whole way down. By the time I got to the canyon, the sky was dark. As I moved back east toward Estes Park, though, it got a little nicer. But stay tuned; it will probably change again. It constantly does in the mountains.

After driving for a little while, I decided to get out of the car and enjoy the altitude again. I parked my car on the side of the road just below tree line and head down the side of the hill. I took my car keys and phone and headed off. I climbed to where the road and my car was out of sight so I could have some privacy.

I finally got a great area to sit on a fallen tree. I could see the peaks through the tall pines, and I still had those majestic trees surrounding me. They were below me, they were to my left, they were to my right, and they were at my back. I was surrounded, and that was just fine. I felt protected.

It was at this exact moment the enormousness of what I had just done and what had just happened filled me from my toes to the top of my head. I felt every inch of my body, and it was released—released from all the stress I was carrying with this heavy responsibility. Again another Aahhhhh! moment. That quickly passed as my sentiment for my loved ones kicked in.

Then as Garth Brookes would say, "Deep in her heart, the thunder rolls." The intensity and somberness of what had just happened hit me—and hit me hard. I sat in those trees and cried, wept, and at times laughed. And I even almost threw up with the nerves that were rattling me. It was a very difficult and solemn moment. And completely unexpected.

I was alone in the trees, sobbing, as people drove by, enjoying this amazing park, and nobody knew I was there. And nobody knew that I was alone. And nobody knew that I had just done the hardest thing, emotionally, that I had had to do alone ever in my life. And nobody knew how much my heart hurt and how I could feel it being ripped apart from how much I missed my dad and Mark.

And nobody knew how I felt like a little girl, lost and scared and not sure what to do next to be honest.

I sat there and let all that I was feeling be felt. I breathed deep the air and let the mountain sweetness fill my lungs and mind. The thunder finally subsided a little, both in me and the sky, as thunder will do, as all things pass eventually.

And I started to marvel at myself. *Look at what you just did. And yes, you had some help, and yes, you had some weak moments. But you did it, and you did it properly even if you really didn't plan it.* But who could have planned all that?

I could still hear the thunder rolling higher up in the mountains through the valley, so I needed to get going. But just for fun, I took out my phone and snapped a picture of the mountains coming through the trees in front of me. And then turned around and took a picture of the sunlight coming through the trees directly behind me.

And guess what!

I got both pictures, and now the phone on my camera worked just fine. Although I was actually just below tree line at about nine thousand feet above sea level, not that much lower than my hike. A peculiar thing indeed. They both were very good photos in fact. The one from the front looking down had a stunning view of the white-capped mountains framed perfectly by big pine trees and aspen.

The one I took directly behind me was a magical shot. The light was streaming in through the trees in such an otherworldly and ethereal kind of way that it was just beautiful! It looked straight off an inspirational calendar. I used it as my profile picture for a while after that. It makes me smile and think that the heavens were with me in that moment and all that day.

It was a good thing I made it down the mountain when I did because it started to rain within an hour of me getting back to my cabin—a hard downpour rain, sheets of rain and deep thunder and a chill in the air of fall. It was a very cleansing rain and exactly what I needed at the time. I love a good thunderstorm, and there is something very comforting to me about them. Maybe it is just the Nebraska girl in me, but they make me more secure than frightened.

Another thought in my head was of the rain up in the mountains where I just hiked. Although at Lake Haiyaha, it was probably coming down as snow, it was still refreshing to know that the ashes and trinkets were being covered with a moisture that would wash them away eventually. They would be fresh and clean and blended into the lake and mountainside rocks where they would become one with the environment and just be. They would get the final kiss from Mother Nature as their souls (in my mind, remember) would go back home. It seemed like the perfect conclusion to the whole theme of the day, and I could not have dreamed of a better way for it to end.

Happy birthday, Mark! Deed done. Crazy how it all happened ...Thank Dad for sending me Nick and singing "Happy Birthday" with me. He said some beautiful things. And thank yourself for sending me the 2015 version of Sven. Andy from, yes, you guessed it, Sweden. I know that was a personal joke and a good one! Hahaha! It really, really showed me that you guys are still with me. You gave me gifts today that helped solidify that notion. That somehow brings me comfort. Still brokenhearted, but I know you guys miss me too. :)

I took a hot shower when I got back and changed into comfy clothes. With this storm, I was definitely in for the night. I made a huge roaring fire; it was my last night before going home in the morning, and I felt obligated to use up the stack of wood that still remained. Plus, with the cold rain, it was the perfect blend. I kept some of the windows cracked so I could hear the rain and thunder though. I heated up whatever was left in the fridge and ate all the perishables I could before leaving the next day. I sat and relaxed by the fire, feeling content.

I was exhausted both physically and, of course, emotionally. I felt satisfied though and enlightened. I really marinated on everything that had happened and tried to commit it to long-term memory. It felt important. But as I said, I was really worn out and depleted.

It just so happened that the Vikings were playing the San Francisco 49ers on Monday night football that night. That seemed so fitting considering it was Mark's birthday and that was one of the things we did together, watch football. I like to think he was with me in the cabin that night, cheering alongside me.

After eating and stoking the fire, I crawled into bed with my TV on football, the fire crackling and the rain tapping at the roof and windows and watched the game. The Vikings ended up losing to the 49ers 20–6. I was asleep before the halftime. I am sure Mark stopped watching it about then too.

I don't remember any dreams or even moving all night. I was as tired as you get that night. I awoke the next morning early so I could make good time on the way back, and I felt like I had slept a full twelve hours. I was awake, excited to share my story with everyone when I got home and happy. There was a feeling of satisfaction that was refreshing.

I packed up the car and my coolers for the ride and got going. I made lunch so I would not have to stop anywhere down the road. Then I pulled away from my cabin. It was going to be a good day for traveling with bright skies and little wind or traffic. It is not a hard drive from Estes Park to Omaha once you wind your way back down from the almost eight thousand feet above sea level you are at. It is boring landscape after you get across the hills, so flat and straight ahead is really the only direction you need to attempt after that.

But it's my home, and I was grateful for every mile I got closer to it.

The drive home was not unusual in any way except I got pulled over by a Nebraska State Patrol officer. It made me a little mad because some truck just flew past me a few miles back, clearly speeding, when I got pulled over. He should have been the one the officer stopped. But I got away with just a warning, so that worked out.

I do not know what it is about being pulled over, but even if you know you are not really in trouble, your heart starts to race! I looked around the car for anything illegal, knowing I did not have anything. It still gets the body going and my hands shaking a little. After my minor nerve-racking stop, I made my way back down the highway, glad the piece of paper he gave me was yellow and not pink.

I made good time, only making a couple bathroom breaks or gas stops. It seemed like a long ride because I was so anxious to get home, but it was the normal eight hours. Finally, I saw the Lincoln State Capitol and knew I was less than an hour away! It is always hard to not speed at that point because I want it to be done and I am so tired by then. At last I was at my exit. I was just a few miles from my home now. It was only a few minutes later that I was hitting the garage door opener and back to my happy place. Home Sweet Home.

Chapter 5
The Dessert

Being loved deeply by someone gives you strength,
while loving someone deeply gives you courage.

—*Lao Tzu*

We made it, my friends, to the sweet end, although in this story, it is more like the bittersweet end—but sweet nonetheless. You have made it to that delicious part where you are full and almost content with your meal. The sandwich was good and was super flavorful. It eventually got to its satisfying taste.

And I still savor this sandwich and get nourished by it when I need to. When the doubt sets in, I try hard to remember the seasoning of that trip. Sometimes I am successful, and sometimes I still let grief and anxiety get their way. But I am getting better. Self-improvement is a lifelong task.

But who doesn't like sweets after their meats? The sweet things in life are what a good and meaningful existence are made up of. There will always be bitter parts in life that we have no choice but to taste. And we will always do our best to make lemonade out of lemons …yadda yadda yadda. That is just our nature.

So pick out your sweetness to end the tale with; if you're a chocolate girl like me, maybe a hot fudge sundae. Or maybe you are a tart or sour-sweets lover. I personally like cake and pies, although I won't turn down a chocolate chip cookie dough ice cream in a sugar cone any time of the year! Whatever is going to satisfy you at the end of a long filling sandwich made just the way you like it. Now treat yourself to whatever would go prefect with that sandwich. Everything in moderation, right? Go ahead. You deserve it.

But when faced with something you do not want to taste, something that chokes you up literally, how do you take that in? How do you take in that taste and be grateful for what it is giving back in return? It is filling you up and nourishing you in some way even if you do not feel it now, even the sugars because we do need those too. That is why you have to leave your eyes and mind wide open. This is also the reason I always eat with the light on. You should face head on what you are taking in and on.

When I walked into the house that evening, I got home and hugged my husband. I started to cry. (Big shock, right?) I was so relieved to be home and safe. I was so emotionally drained and excited at the same time. I was in shock still at everything that had happened and could not wait to tell everyone. But I was all over the place—a bundle of uncontrolled nerves.

My husband sat me down and let me start talking. As I told him of my adventures, I took it day by day. I told him about the signs, and he nodded and was amazed in the right places. He cried, sometimes with me, sometimes alone. He never once doubted what I was telling him. He saw my faith and the peace of mind I had brought back from this trip and was not going to lessen that in any way. At the end of my tale, he told me it was incredible. He said I was very lucky to have my dad and Mark both be with me when I needed them.

I told him how nervous I was to tell my sister, Sandy, and brother Dan, especially since I was near Dan on his birthday and did not let him know. Greg assured me that once they heard this story and all the crazy amazing things that happened, they would not be mad. And if they were, he had my back. That helped me in the confidence I had telling everyone this truly unbelievable story.

I wrote it all down that night so I would not forget anything. I am sure there were things that I did forget or missed the meaning of. But the notes I wrote were amazing enough for me to stare at in awe.

Did this all really just happen? Exhausted, I took a bath and crawled into bed beside my husband, glad to be safely home with the dog, cat, and man I loved next to me again.

I was off work the next day, and I started the day with a trip to my mom and dad's place to see my mom and tell her of all that had happened in Colorado. I was nervous but headed right in the door and told her everything. I was nervous because my mother had a strong religious upbringing and I thought that she might not believe all the psychic, almost magical signs I had seen and felt. She might not have the same spiritual beliefs that I had and that had only gotten stronger in Colorado.

But she was touched and believed right away my story, saying things like "Oh yeah, that was your daddy all right" and was nodding and tearing up, asking questions about my stories. She wanted to hear it all and believed it all, much to my relief. I told her I was nervous to tell Sandy and Dan, but she assured me that they would want to hear it and not to worry about what their reaction would be.

I think my story comforted her as much as it did me. Why did I ever doubt she would believe me? All these experiences were based on our faith, the belief that we will all be united again on the other side, that Jesus and God would protect and help us in our hours of need, that our loved ones still watched over us and could hear us pray to them. I guess it was just that to me, that this whole experience felt supernatural in a way, and that is an area not everyone believes is real.

I was feeling empowered by my mom's reaction and delighted with how it seemed to bring her comfort when I made my next stop. I went over to see my sister and tell her all about it too. We are very close and rarely keep things from each other, so I went, hoping she would not feel betrayed that I did not confide in her what my plans were.

I went inside her house, and she knew instantly that there was something going on. I told you we were close, and she could probably tell I had been crying as well. As I came inside, I had her full attention.

Not knowing how to even start, I took a deep breath and said, "I need to tell you where I just came back from and what I did." As we sat on the couch. "I made a promise to Mark a long time ago that I would spread his ashes in the mountains after he died, and that is what I just got back from doing."

I believe her reaction was "Really?" and she started to tear up.

I told her that I had just got back from telling Mom what had happened and that nobody except her and Greg knew I was going.

I then told her the entire story of my trip, checking my notes so I would not forget anything—right from the guilt and stress of driving out there and then seeing the "L BELL" license plate to the day I spread the ashes. Every little detail I could remember. She was emotional while listening to the story and once again believed me from the start. She was amazed at the things that had happened and helped me to understand them even more. She never once doubted that Mark and Dad were with me on that trip.

She was not mad that I went there alone. She even said she didn't think it was something she could have done. Like my sister always did, she made me feel proud of myself and what I had done for Mark. She understood the immense importance of fulfilling that promise and how extremely hard it was for me. She also understood how incredibly healing and comforting it was to me too.

As I reached the end of the story, she sat crying with me and telling me how wonderful all of that was, how much she loved hearing about it, and that even just hearing about it from me made her feel closer to Mark and our dad. We hugged and wiped our tears and looked at the pictures of them both that she had hanging on the wall.

And she did something I will never forget.

She said to those pictures, "Thanks, guys, for watching over Laurie and helping her on her trip."

I wept so hard because I *knew* that they were listening. I had been changed from my adventure in the mountains, and I knew with sharp clarity that they were with us and that they heard her say those words. I had zero doubt about that fact.

My sister then insisted that we call my brother Dan in Denver and tell him everything. I had expressed to her that I was nervous he would be mad because I did not try to catch up with him on his birthday, but she assured me that she had my back, that if he did get mad, she would defend me. My family always had each other's back, even if sometimes it was against ourselves. We put the phone on speaker and dialed his number.

When he answered the phone, we told him that we had something to talk to him about. I said I would need his full attention and that I wanted him to keep an open mind. I think he was kind of doubtful at first and just said, "Okay …" Then after I knew I had him listening, I started to tell him.

It was very much like how I told my sister and Mom what had happened day to day and the signs and the feelings I had each day. To his credit, he was silent. He listened and did not interrupt or get distracted. He really took in everything I was telling him, and I could hear his reactions at certain points. I could hear him crying. I could hear him chuckle and mutter reassuring tones. He would ask questions only to clarify what I had said.

When I got all done, he said, "Wow, sis, that is really cool."

By then we were all crying. I came right out and asked him if he was mad that I didn't see him on his birthday or let him know I was in Estes Park.

It was my brother's turn to amaze me then. He said, "No, you had to do this, and I understand. We all understand why you had to do it alone."

I grew in that moment because I think I finally understood that family really does get one another, that there is not any other person on earth who would really understand and say what my brother just did. It was sincere, and I glowed from that supportive statement. All the faults and warts and bad fights and anger we had at times—they did not matter. What we had an abundance of to counteract those things were love—true love for one another.

There it was. I had told the most important people in my life, and they all were okay with what I had done. It was exactly like my dad, the king of worriers (from whom I swear I got it from), had always told me. Most of the stuff you worry about does not become anything. It is the stuff you are not worried about that will sneak up on you. You are right as usual, Dad, even if you did not practice what you preached.

I did not tell my brother Steve about it. I was not sure how he would take it. He was actually the one person I thought would doubt what had happened. He would say I was reading signs that were not there or seeing things and making a meaning of things that did not exist. He was very smart and matter of fact, and I was unsure how such a story would be received from such a logical person.

I left it up to my mom to tell him. I know. What a scaredy-cat, right? I just did not want anything to tarnish the feeling I was having from this trip. I knew the world would crush it soon enough, but I was enjoying my Rocky Mountains high for the moment. Truth be told, I love my brother Steve, but we are not as close as my sister and my brother Dan are. Or as close as my dad and Mark were for that matter. Maybe it's the oldest-versus-the-youngest thing. But he is my brother, and I am happy to be his sister.

I did tell a few of my close friends and Mark's best friend, Tony, and his wife. They all were moved by the story and encouraged me to do what I am doing right here: write it down and share it. They convinced me it would give others hope and peace of mind. It is my sincere hope that this is what it does for anyone who reads this and needs it—peace of mind.

So the year continued, and the glow and contentment I felt from that trip dulled as it often does in life. But what happened in Colorado is an amazing thing, and I do want to remember it, which is another reason for writing it down. You are knee-deep in my therapy session with me. To relive it makes me feel it again on some level. It makes me feel close to them again. I have felt my brother and Dad around me quite often since then. I can remember some specific times when I felt them so strong it felt as if I could turn my head and they would be standing right there.

We had Mark's best friend, Tony, and his wife, Darcy, over for Halloween the year following Mark's death, with their twins for trick-or-treating and chili. Their son Josh was particularly close with my brother and still so devastated from our loss. The "boys" would often do things together, and Josh thought of Mark as his uncle, his family, rather than just his dad's friend. We would talk about him together, and he would write me letters and send me drawings of wolves and tell me how much he missed Mark. I would write back and share stories with him. That first Halloween after going to Colorado was a really fun time. We invited my mom over to our party, and my sister and niece came over as well. My great-niece Aurora came with them, so we had adults and kids. And it was a weekend, so it was really a party night. Everybody wore costumes, and it was very festive.

We walked around the neighborhood; it was a beautiful night. The weather was perfect, leaves rustling in the breeze, a spooky atmosphere at the houses, and kids running around, having a great holiday of spooky costumes and candy. One of our neighbors had even staged a werewolf they had "caught" with a man jumping out of a trailer, wielding a chainsaw! It was such a fun night and felt perfect in every way.

As we walked down the street, Tony next to me said, "Do you feel Garzo?"

I laughed and said, "Yeah, I totally do. He would have loved all this."

Then Tony said, "You mean, he loves all of this. He is definitely here with us right now, walking around with us. I can feel him next to me." He was right. Mark was there and having a blast!

This was also Alpine's first Halloween with us, and Greg said he was smiling the whole time as they handed out candy to the kids. He would run out and check them out and then run back inside and wait at the top of the stairs for the next kids to ring our bell. After the kids got back from trick-or-treating, they watched some holiday shows I had recorded and ate some more of Greg's chili. At one point, I went into the living room to see how everyone was doing, and Alpine had crawled on the couch with the twins. When I saw him up there, I asked him what he was doing! He was not allowed on the couch. He just smiled his big goofy grin and snuggled up to Michelle and Josh as if to say, "They said I could come up here." I couldn't help but laugh. I said, "Okay. The new rule is, you can only get on the couch when the twins are over."

And every time since then, when they visited, they coaxed him on to the couch, and he is the happiest dog in the world in that moment!

Our first Christmas without Dad was very difficult, as you can imagine. It had always been such a special holiday for the family. My parents always did their best to make it special. It was a Christmas filled with private tears. The family was together. We were celebrating, but I recall more than one time going into the bathroom and crying. We were comforted with the thought that at least Dad and Mark were together now. But as anyone who has lost someone who was maybe sick or old, the words "It is better this way. They were suffering, and now they are at peace" do not mean anything to you when you are heartbroken. Logic never rules my heart, so in that moment, all I want to say to someone is "No, it is better if I could still have them in my life."

The year played out, and the new year began. We all still saw signs from our loved ones. I still saw birds watching me. I still found pennies and quarters. By now, I have filled up several votive glasses with them. Alpine is still woken and startled out of a sleep by something. If only he could tell us what it was that was waking him up. My mom still has a cardinal that comes around and watches over her in the morning. My sister still sees feathers and rainbows above her when she looks up and in times when it doesn't make sense that there should be a rainbow.

Once, I was over at my sister's, and we were discussing the latest out-of-place sign we had seen, and I told her I was jealous that Dad seemed to send her rainbows. How awesome I thought that was because rainbows are so pretty. And Dad sent her such beautiful signs, like feathers and colorful rainbows. I just got coins from Dad, which was what I complained about. I, of course, was half joking about it, but only half.

On my way home from her place that night, I was driving out on a hilly country road that when you got to the top, you could see for miles in every direction. I was thinking about what I had said to my sister, and when I got to the top of the hill, I looked to my left, and there in the sky was the brightest-colored and thickest rainbow I had ever seen! I remember saying "Wow!" out loud as I drove down the hill. As I drove back up the next hill, I looked again off to my left, where the rainbow was, and nothing. It was gone. I scanned the horizon for any color, and there was nothing. This huge brightly colored rainbow had just vanished. There were not even any clouds in the sky that might be covering it up. It had just disappeared. I drove up and down the hills a couple more times, looking for it again, but never even saw a glimpse of color.

I started laughing in my car then. "Okay, Dad, I got it. You sent me a rainbow because you always spoiled me, and I guess you still are." I called my sister from my car, still heading home, and told her what had just happened. She agreed that Dad was just showing me that he heard me and if I wanted a rainbow, well then, I was going to get a rainbow.

That was the only time I have ever seen a rainbow that should not have been. My sister continues to see them, and I still get coins. But there it is again. I feel it is solid proof that our loved ones are still with us and hear us and love us. They do what they can to communicate with us. We just have to be open to see or hear it. If I close my eyes, I can still see the vibrancy and colors of that huge rainbow, how it filled the entire east sky. It makes me smile and feel content every time.

As time marches on, we all still struggle sometimes with our grief. We all have good days and bad days. On the good days, I smile and laugh and almost feel like myself again. I admit it, I am different than I was before losing my brother and dad. On the bad days, I cry and sit in the dark or go out to the cemetery and just lie on the grave and pray and let the tears fall. I am quick to tears almost all the time and have a hard time dealing with the challenges of life.

I used to be stronger—I know that. But my strength will return at times, and it is in these moments that I am amazed by it. I fell down the dark hole of grief for so long that when I do peek my head out from time to time, it is startling.

I am lucky to have the support of my family and friends to get me through. We have all had loss, and we need to hold one another up from time to time. We talk. We cry and reminisce about the past. We have all turned to coloring as adults as a form of therapy too, taking turns getting one another colored pencils and color books. It is surprisingly calming. And hey, I am all about nurturing the kid inside.

Another thing we did that was important to my mom was, we took some of Mark's ashes out to the cemetery and buried them next to Dad. I still remember my sister, niece, and me going out to the grave site with our shovel in hand. I am sure that was quite a sight to see. We had a wooden cedar box that Sandy had gotten from Mark's house, and we had put some of Mark's ashes in there. We also put a rock that I brought back from the place I spread his ashes in Colorado and some of Alpine's hair. My sister had an angel charm she put in, and we sealed it all airtight to bury. We removed the grass of a little square next to the headstone; the box was only about three inches by five inches and not very deep. After putting the grass square aside, we then dug down about a foot and laid the cedar box inside. We said a prayer and covered it all back up. Once we put the grass back on place, you could not even tell where we had dug.

It was meaningful to my mom to have a part of Mark out there with Daddy. She goes out every Sunday and visits them and puts out decorations or flowers. She had gotten Mark a statue of St. Mark when he was going through his treatment as support. That statue is out there next to the flower vase, attached to the headstone. It is a little statue of only about three inches high, so it snuggles in that spot perfectly. When my mom puts out new flowers or decor, she always places some down by the statue for Mark. I know it brings her comfort to know they are truly together, even on the earth now.

A very significant thing happened to me that really got this book moving along. My niece Angie gave me the most amazing gift I have ever gotten. She gave me a physic medium reading for my birthday. She knew I was really having a difficult time letting go, even after Colorado, so she hoped this would help. I love her for that. Angie and I have always been spiritually linked and shared similar beliefs and feelings about the beyond. I am not sure about your beliefs, but I do believe that there are people who can speak to others that have crossed over. We probably all have the ability, like when you get signs or have "that feeling," but there are just some that have control of it, some that are more in tune to the other side.

I admit I went to that appointment in May with a very nervous stomach. I wanted so badly for it to be real and for me to be able to speak to my dad and brother if only for a brief time. I wanted the session to reassure all the things I had been trying to deal with, that they were still with us, that they still knew what was going on down here in our lives and hear us when we talked to them. I wanted specifics things to be said that were not just a broad stroke—no phony reading and guessing to get information out of me, all those things you typically think of when you think of a con artist.

But my niece had heard good things about this lady and knew someone who had gone to her, so I trusted it would not let me down even if I did feel like I was going to throw up at any time. I was not disappointed. The following are just some of the highlights of the half-hour reading, although I did stretch it to forty minutes. As you know, I have a hard time letting go of the ones I love.

She started the session with a tarot card reading for me and told me I was going through a spiritual awakening in my life and that in order to go through that, I had to be punched in the gut by life and punched hard! Gee, ya think? All in all, she was very excited about my tarot cards and said, "Holy crap! Great cards and a great time in your life right now. Whatever you want to do, go for it, because the universe is lined up for you to get whatever you want or need right now."

I liked the way this was starting!

She then told me she had several people coming through for me and said, "Let's get started because they are yapping in my ear."

I am going to stop right now and set the scene a little for you all.

We were in a cozy office with this lady, behind a desk and beautifully decorated walls and room. It felt like a business meeting in some ways. As we sat across the desk from her, she would look up above us or in the corner of the room and talk to, well, whoever was coming through for her. She would be having a full conversation with them in her head and just says things like "Yeah, yeah, I will tell her" or "Okay, okay, I get it. All right. I will" and then deliver these messages. It was crazy to witness and a little freaky too. She is an over-the-top personality but an attractive woman, kind of soccer mom–looking blonde but cussed like a sailor. I truly believed everything that happened that day was real, and it was amazing and life-changing for me and others. But I must continue before giving away too much.

So then she said, "First off, let's talk about the career. They want to talk about that first. What do you do for a living or want to do?"

I told her I was in retail management and had been for decades and that I liked it.

She said, "No, no, that's not it. They are showing me …What else? What else? What do you *want* to do for a living?"

I said, "Well, I was thinking about writing a book."

And she yelled, "Bingo!" And she pointed at me. "That's it! That's what they are talking about."

She then told me that she was writing a book too and that she had some advice for me and that was one reason I was meant to come in to see her; it was so she could talk to me about my book. She encouraged me to do it and told me some of the tricks she had learned when writing and talked about how to publish my book and what she intended to do about publishing her book.

I was to look for the signs because they were about to come to me tenfold. I would start getting information about book writing or meet an author or editor—signs that, yes, this was what I was supposed to do.

"Just do it," she said, "because this is one of those things that you will be on your death bed and be like 'Dammit! I should have written that book!' It is that important to your path in life. Plus, your intent is good. You want to write this book for other people. You are not just looking for a payday."

That is why I went out the very next day off and bought a little purple laptop to write my book on. It was to be used for that purpose and that purpose alone. And thus, a book was born! As I said before, people are in your life for very specific reasons, and she was in my life on that day for a very special reason. I do believe that.

She then continued on with my reading and said, "Did you lose a sibling?"

And I answered, "Yes."

She said, "And did he serve in the military? Or wait, that's your father. Did you lose your dad too?"

As I started to cry, I nodded my head and said, "Uh-hum." So it had started, and the two people I wanted desperately to speak to where coming through.

She said, "Your dad had blood issues. He said, 'I had bad blood and heart.' But your brother died of cancer of some type, right?" And I agreed. She was correct.

But then she said, "It was different types of cancer, not just one." He was here too. Then she said, "I am sorry. It's loud where they are, and I can hear people playing cards, glasses clicking, and other people in the background. It feels like a real party."

Angie and I both laughed at this. My family always played cards. One of my dad's best friends had died right around this time, and they always played cards when they got together since I was a little girl back in the old neighborhood growing up. We looked at each other and said that, yes, they were probably playing cards.

What she said next was one of those signs I had asked for, something very specific to me that rang home to my heart.

She said, "Your dad says he just got tired. He got tired, and he had to go home." It was just what my dad had told me that last Sunday I saw him when he said goodbye: "Elle, I am ready to go home."

The she said, "But your brother says, 'I didn't quit. My body quit. I was ready to keep fighting.'"

I cry and laughed at this. That *is* my brother—always the warrior, always fighting until the end. His body just could not keep up with his warrior spirit. That was how he saw it, and I agree.

"You were very close to your dad, weren't you? And he is most recent, but your brother hasn't been there long either."

I told her about losing Dad six months after Mark and that it was less than a year ago. She looked in the corner and nodded and said to someone "I'm sorry" very lightly under her breath, but I heard it.

Then she told us, "I think your brother was a catalyst in your dad's crossing over when he did."

I agreed. I confessed that I always suspected they would go pretty close to each other. And she nodded, saying, "Yep, yep, you got it. I want you to know that it literally broke your dad's heart to lose his son," she said, "but that they are together now. In fact, your brother is the greeter up there. Holy crap! He greets everyone up there when they cross over. Your brother is a real sweet guy."

I cried and said, "Yeah, he was the kindest man I knew."

She said, "Oh yeah, he makes sure everyone is greeted and gets to the other side. He is a good guy."

That made me smile, knowing that that part of his personality was still the same on the other side. That was his true spirit.

After another glance at the corner ceiling, she said, "Now the book you are writing is about your dad and your brother, right?"

I was floored. I never told her what the book was about, only that I wanted to write one about my life.

I looked at her and said, "Yes, it's about spreading my brother's ashes for him."

She said, "Because they're talking about it, like 'She's going to write a book about us,' and they are high-fiving and laughing. And they keep telling me to tell you to do it. "Just do it,' they keep saying."

I asked her then, "Were they with me when I went to spread my brother's ashes?"

And she confirmed, "Yes, they were. The whole time. And you saw signs too, they said. Hawks, lots of hawks. And your dad came to you in smells."

Then she made the weeping start, as if it had not already begun, but this was a different level.

She said, "They want to say that they know how hard it has been on you to lose them both but they still come around and they are not going anywhere." As I sat there crying she looked at Angie and said, "And they want to say to you it was your idea to bring her, right?" Angie said yes, and she said, "They want to say, 'Good job! That she will get a lot of answers here that she needs and that she will get some healing from this.'"

And as Angie and I cried and held hands, she said to me, "You should ask for signs. They will bring them to you when you need them. Don't be afraid to ask for a sign when you are having a bad day or hard time and just need some boost. They will bring them so you know they are still there for you."

I asked her what signs I should look for. And she said, "Hawks. Hawks and eagles. But I think that is mostly your brother. Your dad likes to mess with your electricity and comes in smells. He drops a lot of pennies for you too." Now I know from my psychic experience, research, TV, etc., that those are pretty regular signs. So this one was maybe a little suspicious, but the fact that she made Mark's be a hawk, and Dad's be coins felt like more than just a parlor trick.

My parents dressed formally to celebrate.

Then she left-turned from me and said, "Your mom and dad were married a long time, weren't they? He comes to your mom a lot. He says that she is doing okay but that nights are hard for her. He comes to her every night around 3:00 a.m. and sits on the bed or lies down with her. He is around her a lot. He is with her every morning while she does the routines they usually did together."

That made me happy. Their love saw no boundaries. He still loved her and always would. And I hoped she could feel him coming around her. I was already hoping this reading would somehow bring her comfort too.

The psychic told me, "They still talk. She talks to him, and he talks back. She may not hear his voice, but she can hear him. And I will tell you it is real. They are that in love." I was not surprised.

The next thing she said was another validating moment for me.

She said, "Your grandma came to get your brother when he crossed over." She said it very matter-of-factly. But here's the thing. Towards the end, my brother talked about seeing Grandma and not wanting to go with her yet. We all thought it was the drugs talking, and maybe it partially was, but she just pulled that out of the air; she could have said anyone came to get my brother. But my grandma? Too random to not be true, in my opinion.

The validation hits just kept coming.

She then said, "Your grandma is here, and so is another lady, but I cannot understand her. Do you have Czech in your background?"

I said, "No, I have Polish."

A side note: she had no idea what my last name was at this time, which was Travis, or my nationality.

And she said, "That's it. I could not understand this lady because she is speaking Polish, but this must be your other grandma."

"Yea, my dad's mom, my Grandma Victoria spoke Polish all the time," I said.

She replied, "She just wants you to know that she is here too and that you are not alone. I cannot understand what else she is saying …something about a bird. Did she have little yellow birds?"

And I told her that yes, my grandma had parakeets. "That's her."

Then she asked what questions I had. Where to start? Here I was, with a direct connection between my loved ones and me, and what should I say? What would you say if you had one last chance to talk to someone you lost, one last phone call or message to give them? I should have been more prepared. I felt an enormous amount of pressure all of a sudden.

I asked if my brother approved of what I did for him in Colorado.

She looked above me and said, "He says he likes the place you picked. He could not have thought of a better place, very good spot." I was relieved. "They also both said that you needed help, and they both sent it."

I was shocked. I asked, "So that was them that sent Nick and Andy?"

"Of course, it was," she said as if it was obvious. "They said you needed help up there, and they sent it. You needed help, and let's face it, you were not in the best place emotionally. So you needed them, and they came. Them and your guardian angels were also on that trip with you."

I knew it, but now I *knew* it. I am not sure why, but that was a huge validation for me. I did not just make something out of nothing. It validated why I wanted to write this story and share this amazing experience.

Then I asked if Mark thought we were doing a good job with Alpine, his dog.

She said, "Yeah, great job. But he comes around and pokes and teases the dog a lot."

I looked at Angie. I had told her about Alpine jumping up out of nowhere and being surprised or jumpy. We had talked about if he was dreaming or there was something physically wrong. So she knew …We both just stared at each other like *what!*

The psychic then said, "Out of nowhere the dog will just be sleeping, and then he will just jump up like someone just jabbed him, because someone did. It's your brother. And he claps his hands and startles him."

Then I told her that, yes, this was happening. I said, "We even asked the vet what was going on, and he didn't really know. He said there was no physical reason, that maybe he was dreaming or something."

"Nope, it's your brother being ornery," she said.

She had messages for both of Mark's children, which were very personal and which I delivered to both of them. I hoped it helped them heal. I will not get into what was said, but from the message and the verbiage, I know it was my brother. He called Brandon "my son." That is how Mark *always* referred to Brandon: "Son, get me a pop," "Son, call me when you get home." That was what he called him. She could not have found that out from anyone but Mark. Plus, the message would have only been from Mark.

The message she gave for me to give to his daughter Brittany was also one only he would know. I did ask if Mark knew about Brittany's new son, and her comment was "Nice name, isn't it?" which validated the issue for me. Brittany's new son's name was unique and a little controversial at first. It is a name we have all grown fond of now, but at the time, we were all like "What?" The fact that his first message about him was his name was right on.

I was curious to know something, so I asked, "Do they know about the tattoos I got for them?"

She said, "Well, your dad said yeah, but you didn't have to do that. He says it's the thought that counts." This made me smile because whenever I told my dad I was going to get a tattoo for him like I did for Mark, he would always tell me I did not have to do that. He always said, "Sometimes, Elle, it's the thought that counts." So here he was again, saying the same thing. Oh, Dad.

But she said about my brother Mark, "F*@k, yeah, he knows!" This just told me he thought it was as cool as I thought it was. He wouldn't cuss unless he was excited, so I knew he loved it.

She asked me then, "Did your brother have a Harley-Davidson? Or wanted a Harley?"

I answered her, "No, he didn't own one, and I don't think he wanted one."

But she kept insisting that he kept showing her a Harley-Davidson or something.

"He just keeps showing me Harley-Davidson. So did he dress like he owned a bike or something about clothing?"

And Angie and I both said, "Yes, actually, he always wore Harley T-shirts or hats." She said she did not think that was it; it might be. But she told us to think about that because that was not exactly right.

It was not until I got home later that night and went to get changed into my "kick around the house" clothes that I realized what she was talking about. One of the items I took from my brother's house was a T-shirt. A Harley-Davidson T-shirt with a wolf on it. I wear it all the time. I switch it out to wash it from time to time, but I wear it the most. I bet that was what she was talking about—the shirt of his that I wore.

I took two shirts from his house—the Harley one that I still wear and a red, white, and blue tie-dyed shirt that we took for Alpine. He would lie with it and chew on it. It was a comfort to him when transitioning into our home and his new reality. I understood. I kept my brother's shirt next to my side of the bed for a short time when it still smelled of him. I would sniff it and remember the hugs we would give each other and his sweet smile. The sense of smell was very strong and conjured up all kinds of memories and emotions. In those early weeks, Alpine would even squeeze his big body over to my side of the bed in between the mattress and the wall just so he could smell Mark while he slept. It broke my heart, and I would go find his shirt and lay it down by him when he did this.

He eventually chewed up the shirt out of comfort and grief. We would find tie-dyed bits of poop in the backyard as it passed through him. I took what was left of it and had him wear it as a bandana for a while, but he always found a way of getting it in his mouth, and it got too small to wrap around his big neck. I still have what is left of it.

As you can see, the reading was something special. She was right on with the messages given and information she had. It was mind blowing and spiritually satisfying. It brought me back to Colorado and all the faith and knowledge I gained out there and reinforced it again. They gave me personal messages for others that helped them to heal as well.

My half hour was up, but I continued to ask questions. She was kind and would still ask but was dismissing me and moving on to Angie in the nicest way possible. I could not help myself. Here I was, talking to Mark, talking to Dad, having a connection with grandparents I have not seen since I was younger. How could I let it end? So I went a little long. Both Angie and the psychic were very kind about it though.

I had a recording of it that I played for those I knew would appreciate it, those who had a direct message from Mark or Dad and would find comfort in it, which they did. My husband, mom, sister, brother, Mark's close friends—everyone agreed there were some undeniably strange things that she said that only Mark or Dad or my family would know about. It was quite amazing. I felt refreshed again, awake again, moving forward again. It was an experience I can never thank my niece enough for. Thank you again, Angie.

As is the circle of life, exactly one year to the day later, we made the incredibly difficult decision to have Alpine put to sleep. He turned nine years old with us, and his health declined almost immediately. We did all we could to help him be pain-free and healthy, and he was always happy. But one day he was in pain even with the heavy medication we gave him daily, and we knew it was time. He crossed over Rainbow Bridge and into Mark's arms again exactly 365 days from that reading. It is one of the saddest and hardest things I have ever done, and that experience has changed me forever. Alpine, I love you still and miss you every day. You really were the best dog, and it was a privilege for us to be your parents if even just for the last few years of your life. Thank you, Mark, for trusting us with your boy. We know you approved of all we did for him.

I will not get into details because a dog like Alpine deserves his privacy and dignity. But I will tell you this. On the day we took him in, it was very stormy. The skies themselves were opening up and wailing. When we got home, I was sitting by the back window in the living room and crying, missing Alpine already. And when I looked out in to the backyard, wishing I would still see Al back there, I saw an eagle come flying out of our forty-five-foot blue spruce and cruise along the top of the fence. Then went behind the neighbors shed and never reappeared.

I remember yelling, "Holy crap, honey! An eagle just flew out of our tree!"

Then it made me think. Maybe that was Mark letting me know that he got Alpine home okay.

I am sure of it. It was the right decision. I knew it beyond a doubt then.

Chapter 6
The Cherry on Top

Blood makes you related. Love makes you family.
—Unknown

So that's my story. You have the whole sandwich, and I even threw in some dessert for you. Pretty good ending, huh? I bet you were not expecting that. It has been the single most life-changing time in my life. An awakening is what it was, a spiritual awakening, just like I was told.

I hope that you, the reader, got something out of my story. I hope you gained some belief, faith, and relief and learned a little about grief. We are all snowflakes in this journey; no two are exactly alike. But that is the beauty of being a human being, of being an individual.

Yet there are times when we are all the same, and we all come together, like in times of disaster, both man-made and natural. At times of terror and senseless attacks on innocent victims, the human race will put aside differences and help one another. Those are acts of love and kindness and unselfishness that only people can process. Never stop believing in miracles because they happen every day.

You are not alone. That is what I want you to know from this. Just like I *know* it now. And also, *love* is the only thing you take with you when you cross over. All those negative energies you feel while on this planet are only to give you the life lessons that you need to experience, the lessons that will help you learn and perfect your soul so you are ready to go home again someday.

The other thing I would ask you to consider is to look for the signs. They will come to you if you need them. If you lost someone you love, be open to things that don't seem like just a coincidence. Ask yourself why. Why are you smelling your dad's aftershave in the middle of the day at work? Is it there from the one you love because you are having a particular hard time in life and need reassurance that you are on the right track?

Or maybe that amazingly vivid dream you just had about your brother visiting you and telling you he loved you and you woke up feeling his kiss on your cheek—was that only a dream? Or did your brother know you needed a hug and he wanted to assure you that he still was with you so he came to you in your dream?

It has been a learning lesson for me. I learned that sometimes grief can blow a family apart! I have learned that sometimes grief can bring a family closer. I have learned that each death is a different level of grief to each different person, including myself. Death of someone you love dearly is by far the hardest thing you will ever go through in your life—harder than divorce, harder than job change, and harder than all the stresses of the world. It is the final pain.

I call this chapter the "Cherry on Top" for a reason. First of all, cherries have always reminded me of a heart. They were red, shaped similarly, sweet, and the stem always made me think of connection. They need that connection to the root to grow. The heart in my mind was always the connection to the rest of your body, mind, and spirit. The connections were the veins and tubes moving the blood through your body so you'd survive—the roots, if you will.

So now I am going to say it.

Life is a mess! It is hard. It is ugly. It is unpredictable and troublesome. It knocks you down and steps on you. It punches you in the gut when you least suspect it, and it is an anxiety-filled ride for many of us. Life sucks!

Life is amazing! It is precious. It is beautiful. It is deliciously exciting and full of new adventures. It has moments of love and laughter that comes straight from your stomach and make you cry in delight. It has memories of smiles you will never forget. Life rocks!

And dessert is the perfect metaphor for this (last one, I promise) because even the most mouthwatering dessert can be a big mess. I love hot fudge sundaes and banana splits are very popular, but what a mess they are! They are what we call a beautiful disaster, but still a big mess. The ice cream mixes up into a goo, the whip cream melts, you walk away done with ice cream all over you and sticky. But for one moment, there it was. It was gorgeous! It was perfect! It had that delicious, sweet, alluring cherry on top, and it drew you into an awesome experience of eating your untidy yet delectable dessert. That is how life can be.

I thank you for joining me on my therapy session, because that is what this really is. It was my way of coping with the deepest losses of my life, which turned into the most spiritual experience in my life. I needed to tell you all for myself in order for my brain to fully compartmentalize the trauma and my heart to fully absorb the pain. To be honest, I still have moments when it is all hard to believe that those things in Colorado happened. But they did. And they were a message. I had hopes that bringing you along for the ride would help you with whatever you are dealing with or will be forced to deal with in your life.

I would also ask everyone to remember that you do not know what anybody is going through in their lives, so lead with kindness. That clerk at the store may just have found out that her sister is sick, or that customer in front of you may have learned their child is in trouble. Have compassion when they lose their patience or do not treat you like you are the most important person at that moment, because guess what—you are not. As a species, we have to find the love we all naturally have for one another. We are not born with the instinct to hate one another or be angry. We learn it. We can also unlearn it too.

Lead with kindness and love.

I want to end with some quotes I keep in mind, as you can see from my journal entries I have included throughout the book. I think words are very powerful. They have the power to lift you up or bring you down. I try my best to let them lift me up. I am often reminded that when you say or think negative things, that sets your mind up for negative thoughts and thus anxious feelings and worry.

I have also always known that writing things down works for me. I am often surprised by what I am able to write but would never find the nerve to say out loud. Word therapy is real. Writing things down to get them out of your system works for me. I am sure that when I go back and read this again, I will be surprised by what I wrote at times.

I have often kept a journal for a year, and when I go back at the end of the year and reread it, I am surprised by some of the things I've written, the things I worried about that ended up meaning nothing, the anger or delight I felt that has since just diminished. It is always a lesson in who I have become during the year. Sometimes I am so proud, and other times I ask myself, "What I was thinking?" or "Was I even thinking at all?" I have looked at this book as release, as a creative thing I needed to do to move on, heal my soul. And if I help anyone in the meantime, then that's just a bonus.

After 9-11, I did a painting that I think of while doing this project. That painting was all about release of all the feelings I had from that awful day. I remember, as I often do in my creative process, looking at the painting the next day and going, "Wow! I do not remember painting that on there." I truly open up my heart and spirit and just let it flow out. It will be the same for this story, I am sure.

I have to admit. I am kind of excited to go back and read it.

These are some of the quotes I try to remember as I am confronted with my daily struggles or feel lost in life.

> *Sometimes the bad things that happen in our lives put us directly on the path to the best things that will ever happen to us.*
>
> —Nicole Reed

> *You don't have to have it all figured out before you can move forward. Sometimes you have to stop thinking so much and just go where your heart takes you.*
>
> —Unknown

You can't start the next chapter if you keep reading the last.

—Michael McMillan

And my personal favorite is this:

If it doesn't open, it's not your door.

—Unkown

My final lines are that I have done all this for the two men I love and miss every day.

This is for my brother Mark. You really are my hero, and I was privileged and proud to be your little sister. The memories I have of our youth and adulthood are precious to me. We were all robbed of time when you left us so early. Thank you for protecting me and being my big brother. And thank you for trusting us with Alpine. He brought us so much in the time we had him. I wish you had warned us how much we would love him and miss him when he's gone, though. As you often said, "Him's the best."

And this is for my Dad, my rock. I still do not know how I am going through my life without you. There have been countless times I am still shocked that I cannot just call and ask you what you would do if you were me, to hear you call me Elle. From the deep questions to the silly (can a rabbit have a heart attack?), you gave me advise that I still cherish today and the unconditional love that only a true Dad can give. I know that there are a lot of you out there who think you have the best dad. I am sure for you they are. But my Dad was the very best dad on this planet. He was the very best Dad for me.

There is not a day that goes by that I do not wish I could hug both of these fine men again. I love you both very much! Until we meet again …

Afterword

These are my memories as I remember them. Guess what—I am human. So some of the dates and extracts of the story may be incorrect, but it is not with any intention. I have changed names to protect people's privacy as well. Yes, this is a true story, but told by someone who admits that I suffer from a form of PTSD. With all I have been through and how I have had to cope with that, I have been told by numerous doctors that I suffer from a form of post-traumatic stress disorder. So at times the extracts of a situation may have been muffled, but I faithfully told them in the way I remember or was told. It is with the only hope that whoever reads this story is better for it. It came from a good, pure place. Thank you for reading my tale and sticking with it to the very end. Good fortune in all you do and for all those you love!

Postscript: As I was writing this book, I received a phone call from a publishing company, asking if I had gotten the information I requested. I was baffled. I could not remember asking anyone to send me information on publishing. Once again, the universe was pushing me to where I needed to be. Even if I never used this company, it was just a validating moment right when I needed it. I also got a self-publishing book for my birthday from my friend Sandy G. That doesn't surprise me, though; she has always supported dreams.

Laurie Travis
September 14, 2017 (Mark's birthday)

Yes, this is the actual day I finished this book. It's an amazing world we live in, isn't it? I could not make this stuff up.

Ackowledgements

"I want to thank my husband, Greg, for all of his support and help with this book. He has seen it in it's rawest start and will be the one of first to see it in it's final book form. He also contributed some of the beautiful images, including the cover art.

Thank you to my family for their inspiration and love. I am very fortunate to be your daughter, sister, aunt, niece and relative. I have some amazing people in my life and feel very lucky for that, family and friends that I love.

And lastly, thank you as well to Bruce, Andy and the entire Page publishing team for helping me bring my vision to life."

About the Author

Laurie Travis is a lifelong artist whose gifted abilities have been nurtured in many different creative mediums—from drawing, pottery, painting, and custom framing to making candles and writing. She is a lover of the outdoors and an explorer of the mountains and big water. Mother Nature has always been her escape. Born and raised in Omaha, Nebraska, she is the youngest of six children separated by only nine years. She comes from a caring, close-knit Midwestern family whose parents were married for over sixty years and are a powerful example of true love. Laurie began working full-time in an art-supply store following technical college and has worked as a retail manager most of her life. Her instinctive leadership abilities and positive, sensible personality come naturally. She lives in Omaha still with her husband and their rescue pets, a black tabby cat and a mixed Great Pyrenees and Labrador dog.

CPSIA information can be obtained
at www.ICGtesting.com
Printed in the USA
FSHW02n1600140818
51276FS